D0380441

ACCIDENTS IN NORTH AMERICAN MOUNTAINEERING

VOLUME 8 • NUMBER 5 • ISSUE 58
2005

THE AMERICAN ALPINE CLUB
GOLDEN

THE ALPINE CLUB OF CANADA
BANFF

ISSN   0065-082X
ISBN   0-930410-98-X
Manufactured in the United States

Published by
The American Alpine Club, Inc.
710 Tenth Street, Suite 100
Golden, CO 80401

Cover Illustrations
Front: Yosemite search and rescue team member Greg DeMatteo being lowered off the lip of "Mescalito" on El Cap in Yosemite, 2001. A Swedish climber had dislocated her shoulder on pitch 17 of the route the previous evening, and Greg is being lowered to bring food and water to the injured climber's partners after she was raised off the wall.
Back: Yosemite search and rescue team member Mica Dash being raised off "Sunkist" on El Capitan in 2002 with a climber whose partner was injured in a large leader fall on the headwall. The climber's hand was badly burned from the rope when he caught the fall.

Photographs by Lincoln Else, Yosemite Climbing Ranger.

♻ Printed on recycled paper

CONTENTS

SAFETY COMMITTEES 2004

ACCIDENTS IN
NORTH AMERICAN MOUNTAINEERING
Fifty-Eighth Annual Report of the Safety Committees
of The American Alpine Club and The Alpine Club of Canada

This is the fifty-eighth issue of *Accidents in North American Mountaineering* and the twenty-seventh issue in which The Alpine Club of Canada has contributed data and narratives.

Canada: 2004 seemed to be a year where spontaneous rockfall, icefall and avalanches were common. We are starting to notice a decrease in ice on various alpine routes in the Canadian Rockies. Rockfall incidents seem to be on the increase, partly as a result of this phenomenon. We share this problem with Europe, as the Alps are reportedly experiencing the disappearance of many historical north face alpine routes, including the Eiger Nordwand. Fatalities from rockfall occurred on both the north face of Mount Athabasca and on the Abbott Pass approach to Mount Victoria. Various other accidents occurred as a result of holds failure. Climbers are reminded that gravity is not their friend. Neither, it seems, is global warming or erosion!

It is difficult to obtain data from climbing areas in Canada outside of the Canadian Rockies. Parks authorities provide information on a voluntary and non-funded basis. We thank wardens in Banff, Jasper, Yoho and Waterton National Parks for participating in this endeavour. We also thank conservation officers in Kananaskis Country and Peter Lougheed Provincial Park in Alberta.

There are accidents which we learned of in British Columbia, but were not able to obtain sufficient details to include them in the summary. We rarely get reports from climbing areas east of Alberta and wish to encourage individuals or organizations in the eastern Provinces to contact us in future with any details which they can provide for local climbing areas.

We wish to thank the following individuals for their contributions and assistance in tracking down information throughout the year: Burke Duncan, Al Horton, Jeff Hunston, John Scoles, Bradford White, Percy Woods, and special thanks to Dave Stephens for all of his hard work in keeping me up to date and informed.

United States: Just when we think incident rates are stabilizing, along comes a year when the fatality rate goes back up to its highest level. The big storm in Yosemite contributed to the ten fatalities in California. The number of "falling rock, ice, or object," incidents increased. As with last year, many of these (ten) were the result of hand and foot holds coming away, leading to falls. The majority of fatality increases were in California, Colorado, Utah, and Washington. The narratives cover most of these.

The increases in reports from Arizona, Oregon, and Utah are as much due to new reporting sources as they are to the seriousness of the situations. The increase in reports from Washington are attributable more accidents on Mount Ranier and in the North Cascades.

It is worth having a brief review of the incidents on Mount Shasta. First of all, at least thirty percent of the incidents in the "descent" category happened here—mostly in Avalanche Gulch. Matt Hill, lead Climbing Ranger and Avalanche Specialist, sent two photographs of this piece of terrain as a result of my asking about whether I should really count this as climbing terrain. (Go the the Mount Shasta website if you are interested in seeing various photos of routes: www.shastaavalanche.org.) In one image one can count over 20 people on the route. It is like a magnet because of easy access and deceptively easy looking terrain, which is actually a 30 to 40 degree snow chute in the top section, sometimes as hard as ice, that requires mountaineering skills. My guess is that people decide this would be a good place to try out this climbing stuff! First-time ice ax users—one who fell was carrying her ax upside down—lose control on voluntary and involuntary glissades. First-time crampon users—who don't take them off coming down—end up tumbling and spiking themselves. Hill and Eric White (also a climbing ranger and avalanche specialist) reported 15 incidents on this route alone this year. Oftentimes they are not able to provide the ages or level of experience of the individuals, but it is apparent from the incidents that the vast majority are inexperienced. Unfortunately, they contribute to the data in Table III and probably to media bias that portrays climbing as a risky activity.

Joining me this year as an interested "apprentice" is Michelle Shonzeit, who has worked in several parks and is currently stationed at Crater Lake. Welcome aboard!

As mentioned last year, for those interested in gathering with peers to discuss various aspects of safety and risk management, consider attending the annual Wilderness Risk Managers Conference, this year to be held in Salt Lake City from October 27 to 29. (Go to www.NOLS.org for information.)

In addition to the dedicated individuals on the Safety Committee, we are grateful to the following—with apologies for any omissions—for collecting data and helping with the report: Hank Alicandri, Dave Brown, Erik Hansen, Matt Hill, Ned Houston, Al Hospers, Tom Moyer, Steve Muelhauser, Leo Paik, Steve Rollins, Brad Shilling, Michelle Shonzeit, Robert Speik, Eric White, all individuals who sent in personal stories, and, of course, George Sainsbury.

John E. (Jed) Williamson
Managing Editor
7 River Ridge Road
Hanover, NH 03755
e-mail: jedwmsn@sover.net

Edwina Podemski
Canadian Editor
700 Phipps McKinnon Building
10020-101A Avenue
Edmonton, Alberta T5J 3G2
e-mail: cwep@compusmart.ab.ca

CANADA

FALL ON ICE
Alberta, Banff National Park, Cascade Mountain, Cascade Waterfall

On January 3, a party of two was climbing on Cascade Waterfall (300 m. III WI3). Sometime between 1500 and 1600, the victim was leading final moves of the last pitch when he fell, injuring his ankles. His partner lowered him to the belay and they decided to retrieve ice screws before starting the descent. Some time was spent retrieving gear and the lowering out was slow. About 1800, the party used their cell phone to call one of their wives, who in turn contacted Warden Dispatch. A warden rescue party climbed to where patient was located below the first set of anchors. The preliminary survey indicated injury to the right ankle, but the patient was comfortable enough to continue with lowering out. Wardens set up a first lower of 100 metres, to the second rescue party, then a second lower of 150 metres to the base of the climb. The patient was loaded into the wheeled stretcher and wheeled to his personal vehicle. His climbing partner drove him to the hospital where he was diagnosed with a hairline fracture of his talus. The rescue was done at night with air temp at –32 EC. The moonlight was a big help.

Analysis

Lead falls while ice climbing often result in fractures to the lower limbs. In cold weather when the days are short, it is important to start early in the day so that there is some spare daylight in case something doesn't go well. The party may have underestimated the time that a series of lowers would require. (Source: Bradford White, Banff National Park Warden Service)

FALL ON ICE
Alberta, Banff National Park, Mount Bourgeau, Bourgeau Right-Hand

On January 4, a party of two was climbing Bourgeau Right-Hand (310 m. IV WI 4R). This climb is often very thin on the first two pitches and difficult to protect. The leader was climbing second pitch and took a lead fall six metres above his third screw (clipped in with a screamer). The screw held but he was unsure if the screamer deployed. The leader fell about 15 metres and injured both ankles. One ankle was severely fractured. The party self evacuated to the Sunshine Ski Village parking lot. In addition to the fractures, the leader suffered frostbite to all toes, but no long term damage is expected.

Analysis

Lead falls with crampons frequently result in lower leg fractures. In this instance the party was concerned that they would be responsible for the cost of a rescue, so did not call for help. Rescue services are included in

Canadian National Parks as a benefit of purchasing a Park Pass and there is no additional charge. With fractures, where there is possible circulation impairment, there is a potential for irreversible limb damage and time may be of essence in obtaining advanced medical care at a treatment hospital. (Source: Bradford White, Banff National Park Warden Service)

AVALANCHE
Alberta, Banff National Park, Mount Wilson, Midnight Rambler
On February 12, John Miner, Jim Andrues, and Russ Howard were climbing Midnight Rambler (240 m. III, WI3) on Mount Wilson in Banff National Park. Two of the three were highly experienced mountaineers and members of the Tacoma Mountain Rescue Unit (WA).

They were hit by a size 2.5 avalanche initiating from a start zone high on the mountain. This likely occurred in the early afternoon. They were carried to the runout at the base of the route and were all buried from one to four metres deep. The three ice climbers were part of a larger group. Other members of the group who had been climbing elsewhere became worried as darkness fell and drove to the trailhead for the climb around 1900. They hiked up to the base of the climb and found avalanche debris and sections of climbing rope coming out of the debris. They searched the deposit and none of the climbers were visible. The buried climbers were not wearing beacons. The search party returned to the highway and reported the accident at the Saskatchewan Crossing Warden station. Park wardens from Banff, Lake Louise and Jasper including two dog teams searched the debris until 0:00 the following morning. One victim was located and dug out. The search resumed at 0700 that morning. The park rescue helicopter was brought in along with more park wardens. The other two climbers were located and dug out later that morning.
Analysis
When they left to start the climb, temperatures were below freezing at the base of the route. Unfortunately, they were not aware that there was a temperature inversion and that at the elevation of the starting zones, temperatures were at or above freezing. When the rescue team responded at night, the residual avalanche hazard from above was evaluated. Temperatures had dropped to an acceptable level and remained below freezing at the start zone elevation the next morning as well. It is unknown if, at the time of the accident, they were still climbing up or if they were on their way down. The temperature inversion conditions could not have been easily being predicted. It is fairly common for ice climbers to not use avalanche beacons. Beacons would not have made any difference in the outcome in this case. (Source: Percy Woods, Banff National Park Warden Service and Tacoma Mountain Rescue)

AVALANCHE
Alberta, Banff National Park, Mount Rundle, Professor Falls

On March 23, a party of two was climbing Professor Falls (280 m. III WI4) and had just finished the technical lower pitches. They were walking roped together towards the last pitch. The second on the rope, T., heard a sound and looked up to see a large avalanche coming over the cliffs above. The two ran to the side of the gully and T. wrapped the rope around a tree a couple of times. The sky went dark gray and the avalanche poured over the two for what seemed like several minutes. T. could look back and see debris piling up where they had just been. The debris pile was over ten metres deep. After the slide stopped, the other member of the team, J., tried her cell and got through to Warden Dispatch. They reported the avalanche and the fact that there were at least three people below them on the waterfall. They then went to look down and determine what may have happened below. Wardens dispatched a helicopter and dog team and prepared for further rescue response. Meanwhile, J. called back on her cell and reported that she was in voice contact with the party of two beneath her and that they were only slightly dusted. J. indicated that they were descending a snow ramp where there had been an ice climb just minutes previously. By helicopter and cell communication, wardens were able to determine that all of the climbers on the route were accounted for and were descending.

Analysis

The avalanche was a Size Three, Natural Slab approximately 60 centimetres thick by 200 metres wide by 600 metres long. There had been no overnight freeze, the temperature was +10 EC at the base of the climb, there was light rain falling in the start zone, and the avalanche danger was rated as "Considerable rising to High with predicted daytime warming." Ice climbs frequently form beneath large avalanche prone bowls. Above freezing temperatures and rain are two of the major contributing factors in ice-climbing avalanche incidents. (Source: Bradford White, Banff National Park Warden Service)

FALL INTO CREVASSE—UNROPED
Alberta, Jasper National Park, Mount Athabasca, North Glacier

On April 9, a party of three were ascending the North Glacier on Mount Athabasca on skis, on a route a little higher than where the "standard" route normally goes. Their intent was to do some skiing as they had done a week prior. At 1310, the party was paralleling a crevasse as they were nearing the top of a roll in the glacier, when K.F., who was in lead, dropped into the crevasse. The party was unroped, unharnessed, and unfortunately, K.F. had the rope. The two friends got as close as they safely could to the crevasse to try to establish contact, but no voice contact could be made. Knowing they could not do much without a rope, they quickly skied down the mountain and dialed 911 from the Columbia Icefields Centre pay phone. Meanwhile K.F. was able to move in the tight quarters just enough to dramatically improve his fight against succumbing to hypothermia. He was able to slide off his pack and get his wind stopper, toque, and balaclava on. He put his down coat next to his chest and with one hand (the other was numb), he managed to get a prusik around his chest so it was ready to clip by the rescuers. Jasper dispatch was notified and a helicopter was brought in. Rescue teams were assembled from Jasper and Lake Louise. Crevasses were fairly obvious from the air and the serac hazard was deemed to be reasonable. It took approximately one hour and 15 minutes for the first party to get on scene from the time of the report and two hours to complete the extrication. By that time, K.F. had spent four hours in the crevasse. By 1744, K.F. was packaged and flown out with a Jasper Public Safety Warden. By 1806 all personnel were off the glacier. At 1841, K.F. was flown with a paramedic to Banff Mineral Springs Hospital and released later that night with no injuries.

Analysis

The party had over estimated the quality of the snow cover on the glacier and choose to travel without a rope or harness on. The team climbed to a high point of a roll to get a better ski run down. Crevasses and localized scouring of snow are common near crests of rolls in glaciated terrain. The team did not see the depression of the snow indicating a crevasse until after K.F. had fallen in. The Rockies snowpack is often thinner and more variable than other mountain ranges to the west. It is rare when conditions exist for traveling unroped. (Source: Al Horton, Jasper National Park Warden Service)

FALL ON ROCK, CLIMBING ALONE AND UNROPED
Alberta, Peter Lougheed Provincial Park, Mount Brock

On April 24, a helicopter spotted the body of C.N. (31) in rough terrain at 8,400 feet in a gully on Mount Brock in the spectacular Opal Range in Peter Lougheed Provincial Park. C.N. was a climbing enthusiast who made a number of climbs in the U.S., Australia, France, and many other areas of the world. A rescue worker had to be lowered from the helicopter with ropes and a harness to recover the body. C.N. died as a result of major traumatic injuries he sustained in a fall of about 1,000 feet. It appeared from footprints that C.N. reached Brock's 2,902-metre peak before falling on the descent. A search for C.N. had been launched after he failed to return from what was supposed to be a day-long climb on April 22. Rescue personnel scoured Mount Brock and nearby Mount Blane, where C.N. began his solo ascent. C.N.'s vehicle was located in a parking lot near the trailhead shortly after police received the call from the family. A helicopter assisted personnel searching on the ground. Conservation officers used scopes to check for any activity on the slopes. The air search was cut short on April 23 due to strong winds but resumed early on April 24. C.N. was familiar with the area, and was in Canmore/Kananaskis to make various climbs. (Source: Burke Duncan)

Analysis

C. N.'s death is the fourth solo climbing fatality in the park in two years.

FALLING ROCK
Alberta, Kananaskis Country, Mount John Laurie (Mount Yamnuska)

At the same time as they were searching for C.N. on Mount Brock on April 23, the conservation officers were called to a rescue on Mount Yamnuska about 1300. A climber was fixing a project, (climbing route) he was working on and a block fell and hit him. The rock knocked him off his stance. He hit the belay ledge eight feet below him and broke both his lower limbs in the ankle area. The hurt climber was able to call 911 on his cell phone. He then lowered himself down from the scree slope. He was slung out by helicopter. (Source: Burke Duncan)

Analysis

Spontaneous rockfall and hold failure is common in this area because of the nature of the rock in combination with the winter melt and freeze conditions. This is evident in the large scree slopes below the crag. For that reason it is imperative that climbers be alert for rockfall and holds be tested before fully weighting them.

RAPPEL ERROR, NO BACKUP, NO HARD HAT
Alberta, Kananaskis Country, Barrier Mountain, Barrier Bluffs

On April 30, a climber fell 15 to 20 metres to the ground while rappelling off a 5.8 sport climb, at Barrier Bluffs, "One Way to Wangland." The 30-year-old climber had finished leading the pitch and had rigged the rope to rappel and clean the route. The figure-8 device he used to rappel with was loaded incorrectly and he failed to test it before committing his weight to the rope. He subsequently fell directly to the ground, hit shoulder first and rolled five metres downslope, coming to rest on a rock. He was not wearing a helmet. Five other climbers immediately lowered off their respective climbs and ran to give assistance. One climber took a cell phone and headed to the road where he flagged down a car for help. Luckily, two registered nurses from the emergency department at the Calgary Foothills Hospital were in the car. They quickly made their way to the accident scene to assist. They performed a detailed assessment and determined that the victim's femur was shattered and that he had ruptured a vein or artery in the upper leg. He had also sustained a compound fracture to the elbow and radius, internal injuries and a number of deep lacerations on his head and body. When they arrived, the victim was bleeding heavily. The nurses repositioned the man so that his blood was going to his head and heart. This action likely saved his life. A paramedic and conservation officer also arrived on the scene within minutes and began preparations to evacuate via helicopter. Alpine Helicopters from Canmore dropped a public safety officer to the scene and went to the road to wait. STARS air ambulance was called and met the helicopter at the highway. A short line and jenny bag were employed to transfer the victim to the highway in serious condition. Two minutes later, a STARS helicopter picked him up and took him to Foothills Hospital. (Source: Burke Duncan)

Analysis

The climber who fell was experienced. He said he had done this hundreds of times and this time he must not have been concentrating. It has become common practice to attach a sling from one's harness with a prusik knot in the rope below the lowering device as a backup.

FALL ON ICE, INADEQUATE PROTECTION
Alberta, Jasper National Park, Mount Andromeda, Practice Gullies

On June 4, two climbers left the climber's parking lot at 0500 enroute to the Practice Gullies (III) on Mount Andromeda. These inappropriately named gullies are similar in difficulty (45 to 55 degrees) and are located on the extreme left hand part of the Northeast Face. They are often capped by large cornices. The climbers arrived at the base and began climbing around 0800 on good snow in the shade of the mountain. They moved quickly up four pitches and then anchored to the rock wall. The snow was thinning out and they were moving out through an interface onto ice. The leader set out, and about four metres into the ice climb, his tool placements failed and he fell. No protection was in place yet and the full force of the fall came upon the belay device that was attached directly to the anchor. It is uncertain what broke or pulled, but the anchor failed and both climbers fell to the base of the climb. A.T. sustained a dislocated shoulder and fractured femur, while his partner C.G. suffered only minor bruising.

A guided climbing party on the Athabasca AA Col route witnessed the fall and sent two climbers down to assist the victim. The guide contacted the Jasper Warden Service via radio and a heli-sling rescue operation was initiated. A total of three wardens were slung into the location where the patient's injuries had already been immobilized. Due to a large overhanging cornice above the route, the rescue emphasis concentrated on a fast heli-sling evacuation of all people.

Analysis

The leader was moving through a difficult snow/ice interface where his tools were not secured in the ice below the snow. When the climber fell, the full force of the fall came upon the anchor through the belay device. The belayer was attached to the anchor separately from the belay device and was not able to absorb some of the forces of the fall. A static belay may have transferred the full force of the fall on to the anchor and overloaded it. It is interesting to note that the rope was not cut and that the belay device and carabiner were not found on the rope. This indicates that the carabiner and/or the anchor line failed, allowing both climbers to fall. (Source: Al Horton, Jasper National Park Warden Service)

AVALANCHE OR ROCKFALL
Alberta, Banff National Park, Mount Deltaform, Supercouloir
On June 5, two climbers in their early 20's were reported overdue attempting the Supercouloir route (IV 5.8) on the North face of Mount Deltaform, near Lake Louise, two days after leaving to bivy for the climb on June 3. The experienced climbers had planned to leave for the climb on Thursday afternoon, spend the evening near the base and start their climb at midnight so they could complete it while the face of the mountain was the most stable. The Supercouloir is considered a difficult alpine route and is located in a relatively remote area at high elevation where avalanches persist, especially during warm sunny days. Based on the description the climbers' friend gave to wardens, the route (under normal conditions) would have been within their technical capabilities.
Analysis
An aerial search was begun and Park wardens were able to trace tracks of the climbers up to the crux exit rock chimneys. The tracks then indicated that the pair had started to descend, possibly due to the large cornices hanging over the exit route. At the 9,900 foot level, ice tools were located on a traverse line on the route. It appeared that the two had fallen from this point.

Park wardens searched the avalanche debris at the base of the route with two dog teams in June but search efforts were suspended due to dangerous conditions on the mountain. The bodies were located visually below the bergschrund a month later on July 5 after some melting occurred. (Source: Percy Woods, Banff National Park Warden Service)

FALL ON ROCK, FAILURE TO TEST HOLDS
Alberta, Kananaskis Country, Mount John Laurie (Mount Yamnuska)
A climber fell and broke his leg on June 5. The man was climbing a route called The Bowl (145 m. 5.10a) when he grabbed onto a chalk-covered handhold that he had used before in a previous climb near the top of the route. The large rock came loose and hit him, crushing his leg and throwing him off the wall. His belayer caught him, but he still fell about 20 metres. A sling rescue was arranged with Alpine Helicopters. (Source: Burke Duncan)

Analysis
The Yamnuska crag has been described by some as a "hopeless pile of garbage rock." There is plenty of good rock to be found on the crag, but it is important to test holds before committing to them.

FALL ON ROCK, NUT/CHOCK PULLED OUT
Alberta, Banff National Park, Tunnel Mountain, The Shoe
On July 6, R B. was part of an "Advanced Mountain Operations Course" being run by the Canadian Military out of CPC Trenton. The group consisted of 14 students and seven instructors. R. B. was part of a group that was learning to lead climb. He had done some top-roped leading practice and a "couple of other easy climbs on lead." He was on the first pitch of "The Shoe" (I, 5.6) on Tunnel Mountain and had placed one tricam about five metres up from the belay. As he neared the traverse left into the crack, he slipped and fell. His gear pulled and he landed on his head on the belay ledge. He then tumbled down below the belay. His instructor called 911 on his cell phone and then began to lower the victim.

The patient was located by rescue on the scree below the climb, still tied in to the rope. He had suffered a severe blow to the head and was displaying wild aggression and thrashing around. There was no response to verbal or pain stimulus only incoherent verbiage and yelling. EMS administered IV and drugs and the patient was heli-slung directly from the scene to the hospital and shortly afterwards transferred to Calgary via STARS air ambulance.

Analysis
The leader was wearing a helmet which was crushed and broken. Dispatchers for 911 in the Banff / Lake Louise area are based in Calgary. Climbers in the National Parks should be aware of the lack of knowledge of the terrain that the 911 dispatchers have and be very clear of their location and the requirement for a mountain rescue response when reporting an incident. (Source: Bradford White, Banff National Park Warden Service)

FALL ON ROCK, INADEQUATE BELAY, INEXPERIENCE
Alberta, Banff National Park, Grotto Canyon, Paintings Wall
On July 18, a climber who fell roughly 30 feet off a wall near the pictographs at Grotto Canyon was rescued. J.G. (51) was leading a 5.9 climb at Grotto Canyon when he slipped and fell 30 feet. He hit a large boulder, bounced off it, then hit the ground, sustaining multiple injuries. A nurse who was nearby did initial first aid, then she ran to the road to call 911 on her cell phone, as there is no coverage in the canyon.

The man had head injuries and had been unconscious for at least one hour by the time that rescuers arrived. He also had irregular shallow breathing, accompanied by gurgling noises, so he was given oxygen. A tricky maneuver executed by Alpine Helicopters pilot Paul Maloney helicopter allowed J.G to be slung out of the canyon. He was then stabilized and transferred to Calgary via the STARS air ambulance. Although he was in critical condition on July 18th, he was in stable condition the following day.

Analysis

Bystanders described the accident as being due to an inattentive or inexperienced belayer who had left too much slack in the rope. (Source: Burke Duncan)

STRANDED, EXCEEDING ABILITY
Alberta, Banff National Park, Mount Rundle

On July 29, a solo climber was ascending the normal scramble/hiking route on Mount Rundle. He scrambled up a gully above trail into the steep technical rock slabs and could no longer go up or down. He eventually managed to attract attention by screaming and someone phoned in to report his location. A warden rescuer heli-slung to the site, placed the stranded individual into a screamer suit and evacuated him to the base of the mountain.

Analysis

While not a climbing incident (thus not included in the statistics), this is a very common occurrence. Inexperienced people often end up on stranded in terrain which exceeds their abilities. Terrain from below often looks easier than it is and it is easier to climb up than descend. Parks has developed detailed route descriptions of the popular scrambling/hiking ascents in the vicinity of Banff to try and prevent people getting off route. These brochures are in French and English and are made available to as many of the local staff and visitor centres as possible. This individual had not seen one, however. (Source: Bradford White, Banff National Park Warden Service)

STRANDED, EXCEEDING ABILITIES, FAILURE TO FOLLOW ROUTE
Alberta, Banff National Park, Mount Temple, Aemmer Couloir

On July 31, a group of four climbers set off to climb the Aemmer Couloir variation of the East Ridge of Mount Temple in Banff National Park near Lake Louise. The group bivvied below the couloir and took the whole second day to climb to the top of the couloir. After another night's bivy, two of the climbers decided they could not continue and the second two went to finish the climb. They would request assistance for their stranded friends. It took them 16 hours to reach the summit ridge after going off route through the Black Towers. Another party who started early that day met up with the two climbers stranded at the bivouac at 1000. They said that they would report the incident to the park wardens. They exited the correct Black Towers exit gully and in so doing bypassed the other two who were off route. The second party reported the incident to the Park Warden Service around 1800. The rescue crew was able to do a partial landing at the bivouac site and evacuate the two climbers. The other two members of the party were then located just exiting the Black Towers on the Summit Ridge. They were exhausted and were evacuated by heli-sling.

Analysis

The East Ridge of Mount Temple is often underestimated. The grade/rating of IV 5.7 is deceptive. The difficulties lie in route finding and mixed alpine terrain for over 5,000 feet of climbing. (Source: Percy Woods, Banff National Park Warden Service)

FALLING ROCK
Alberta, Jasper National Park, Mount Athabasca, North Face

On August 15 at 0530, four Calgary-based climbers started their ascent up the trail to Mount Athabasca's north face. The overnight low at 2,350 metres, recorded at a nearby weather station, was 9.5 C. At 1030, the party of four were at the bergschrund below the north face. N.B. (23) and F.L. (30) started to solo the route while the remaining two, T.R. (24) and J.M. (26) started simul-climbing with running belays. After ascending approximately 110 metres, the group encountered rockfall. At this point N.B. and F.L. roped up. The group continued their ascent and a short time later encountered more rockfall with very large blocks.

The leader, J.M., and T. R. were struck by the rocks and fell approximately 40 metres. Being much lighter, T.R. was pulled upward seven metres towards their ice screw running belay. During the incident J.M. sustained a life-threatening compound fracture of the femur. T.R. sustained significant internal injuries. F.L. and N.B. immediately came to the assistance of their friends, lowering them two pitches to the base of the route. By this time J.M. was reported to have the symptoms of hypovolemic shock and was drifting in and out of consciousness. F.L. ran down the glacier to get help. Parks Canada staff at the Icefields Centre noticed a single person running down the glacier waving his arms, so they called the Warden Dispatch office, which started to assemble a rescue team. At 1245 F.L. contacted the Jasper Warden Service from a phone at the Columbia Icefields Visitor Centre by which time a helicopter was already on standby in Canmore, Alberta. A rescue was initiated and at 1430, a rescue team arrived and started to evacuate the three remaining climbers. By this time J.M. had already died from his injuries. T.R. was transported to hospital for treatment.

Analysis

At this time of year it is not uncommon for freezing levels to remain above 3,200 metres (10,500 feet) in this area. Under such circumstances any route with mixed rock and ice terrain below this elevation is subject to rockfall exposure. Many of the classic routes on the north face of Mount Athabasca have this type of terrain above with the exception of Silverhorn. Compounding this problem is the unprecedented extent and rate of melt-off that has taken place over the past five years in this area. These factors necessitate careful evaluation as to the probability of rock and icefall on any given morning. With daytime warming, the likelihood of rockfall increases. Therefore, by completing a route early in the day you reduce the probability of rockfall. It is not uncommon for persons to do the approach to the glacier in the dark which requires a 0330 start, putting them at the toe of the ice for first light at 0530. It is not uncommon for climbers to be off the route by 1130. (Source: Al Horton, R.Wedgwood, Jasper National Park Warden Service)

FALL ON ROCK, INADEQUATE PROTECTION
Alberta, Banff National Park, Tunnel Mountain, Gooseberry
On August 26, a lead climber in a party took a 30 to 40 foot lead fall on third pitch of Gooseberry (II, 5.6) on Tunnel Mountain. He sustained a back injury but was still mobile. The party rappelled to the ground and started walking out. On the way out the leader started to suffer muscle spasms and was unable to continue. His partner contacted Park Wardens who responded with a wheeled stretcher team. They wheeled the patient out using vacuum mattress immobilization. Subsequent examination revealed a stable fracture of the sacrum.
Analysis
A warden team on a training climb on the same route was about three pitches up and observed the party starting below them. They continued to the top and were unaware that a fall had occurred. The spot where the climber fell had several bolts placed, which make the climb safer and easier to protect than earlier ascents and should prevent a long fall. It is unknown if the leader used the bolts, but subsequent ascents showed them to be intact. (Source: Bradford White, Banff National Park Warden Service)

FALL ON ROCK, FAILURE TO TEST HOLDS
Alberta, Kananaskis Country, Mount John Laurie (Mount Yamnuska)
On September 8, a climber who had been bolting stations on an unnamed route on Mount Yamnuska fell approximately 40 feet , fracturing his ankle. He fell on the fourth pitch while rope-soloing onto a cam. The fall was initiated by a hold breaking. Of particular note was that this was the same person who was involved in the incident reported on Mount Yamnuska on April 23. He had recovered from his double ankle fractures and this was reportedly his first time out since that incident. (Source: Burke Duncan)
Analysis
This is the third climbing incident on Mount Yamnuska due either to rockfall or hold failure this season. In addition, there was at least one serious scrambling incident on this mountain due to rockfall.

FALL ON ROCK, HANDHOLD CAME OFF—FAILURE TO TEST HOLDS, UNROPED
Alberta, Waterdog, North D'art Area, Obliteration

On November 13, B.P. and T.M. were approaching the ice climb Obliteration (30 metre WI4) in the North Drywood area between Waterton National Park and Pincher Creek. The approach involves a 45-minute hike from the vehicles, followed by a moderate class 3 scramble in order to reach the base of the climb. The two climbed up through some easy cliff bands to a ledge below the falls and stopped to have a snack and decide which side to climb (Obliteration or The Gasser). They elected on Obliteration, so they put on their helmets and continued scrambling up the cliff bands with T.M. in the lead. Soon after, T.M. let out a holler and B.P. watched as T.M. fell backward past him. T.M. landed on his back, bounced, and then tumbled down the slope and over the cliff bands, falling approximately 100 feet before coming to rest on a steep scree slope above more cliff bands. As it turned out, a handhold that T.M. was using to pull himself up came loose, causing T.M. to fall backwards. While T.M. lay motionless, B.P. carefully down-climbed the cliff bands to reach T.M. As B.P. got closer, T.M. began to move. While still down climbing, B.P. tried to get T.M. to not move, fearing that T.M. might slip again and fall over more cliff bands. B.P. got below T.M. and began to assess his injuries. They determined that nothing was broken, but T.M. had some major bruising and a sprained ankle.

With the help of ski poles, B.P. and C.G., T.M. was able to walk out toward the truck. The 30-minute descent took approximately two hours. To B.P.'s knowledge, T.M. only suffered major bruising and a sprained ankle.

Analysis

The Waterton area is notorious for loose rock. B.P. noted that two things helped save T.M. from very serious injury. One was the 30 pound pack on his back and the other was his helmet. T.M. was lucky to have stopped where he did. If he had continued rolling and bouncing over the rest of the rock ledges it would have been a much more serious rescue. (Source: Dave Stephens)

FALL ON ICE, UNROPED
British Columbia, Haffner Creek Canyon

February 15, I.T. was solo climbing a mixed route in Haffner Creek Canyon to set up a top rope for friends. He was approximately twenty feet up when he slipped and fell to the ground landing at an awkward angle on his left ankle. Two ACMG guides that were working close by and witnessed the accident radioed Kootenay Park wardens to initiate a rescue response. I.T. was transported via heli-sling to the Haffner Creek trailhead. He was then evacuated by helicopter to the hospital in Banff. I.T. had fractured his ankle in three places.

Analysis
Solo climbing is unforgiving. Slips and even short falls while wearing crampons can lead to serious injuries. (Source: Percy Woods, Kootenay National Park Warden Service)

AVALANCHE, WEATHER
British Columbia, Yoho National Park, Mount Stephen, Super Bock
On March 6, three ice climbers were approaching the bottom pitch of a route called Super Bock (180 m. III WI5) on Mount Stephen in Yoho National Park. Two of the climbers were in a protected location near the base of pitch one; the third climber was approximately ten metres behind them. A wet avalanche poured down the route and swept the third climber approximately 300 metres down slope and into some sparse trees. He sustained a lower leg fracture and significant bruising. His friends quickly responded to his aid and one carried on down to the CPR tracks below and headed to the town of Field to report the accident. The reporting person was able to flag down an eastbound freight train. With assistance from the two CPR staff on board, the climbers were able to move the patient on to the train. They met an awaiting ambulance 1.5 kilometres up the rails.

Analysis
Temperatures had been above freezing for a few days with intermittent rain showers up as high as the avalanche start zones above Super Bock before the accident. Evidence of recent wet avalanches was apparent on adjacent slopes. Above freezing temperatures and rain are two of the major contributing factors in ice-climbing avalanche incidents. (Source: Percy Woods, Yoho National Park Warden Service)

CORNICE COLLAPSE, AVALANCHE
British Columbia, Yoho National Park, Mount Vice President
On April 9, an American man who was backcountry skiing in Yoho National Park died when he was swept away by an avalanche. Park wardens discovered the man's body at about 1800, buried under about 60 centimetres of snow. He had been skiing on the Vice President, a popular destination for backcountry skiing and mountaineering in the Little Yoho Valley. The victim was standing apart from his party on top of a cornice when it broke off. The human-triggered cornice failure produced a size three avalanche on an east aspect starting at 3100 metres and running full path. The slab stepped down to the rocks with the crown over a metre deep in some places. The victim was carried more than 600 metres down the mountain. The party, comprised of five or six members from both the U.S.A. and Canada, had a satellite phone and was able to call for help. Six wardens and two rescue dogs were called to the scene. A helicopter with an avalanche beacon suspended below it was used to locate the victim.

Analysis

At the time of the accident, the avalanche forecast was low but contained specific reference to increasing instability resulting from daytime warming. The forecast warned skiers that large cornices are starting to fall apart. This cornice failure occurred in the afternoon. The same day, a number of other natural avalanches were observed on sun-exposed slopes, demonstrating the deterioration of the snow pack that occurs in the afternoons with spring weather. In the spring, skiers are well advised to get up very early to enjoy the best conditions and finish their ski day early before afternoon warming creates isothermal conditions. (Source: Geneviève Svatek, Banff Crag and Canyon)

FALL INTO CREVASSE, UNROPED
British Columbia, Glacier National Park, Deville Glacier

On May 6, B.E. (48) fell 60 feet to his death in a crevasse in the Selkirk Mountains while ski touring on the Deville Glacier in Glacier National Park. B.E. and four male friends from Canmore were traversing from Battle Abbey to Rogers Pass when the accident happened. The five skiers were doing a variation of the classic Bugaboos to Rogers Pass ski traverse, described in Chic Scott's book *Summits and Icefields* as one of the most magnificent in western Canada. It was a route the experienced B.E. had done twice before. The five had left Canmore on May 1, and were two days short of completing their week-long expedition when the accident occurred. B.E., who was in the lead, noticed the crevasse and when he went to check it for the safety of the group, he fell. A fellow climber rappelled down the crevasse to aid B.E., but he could not find a pulse. Two members of the party hiked down the mountain and contacted wardens by May 7, while two others stayed at the site. The two who stayed on the mountain were airlifted by helicopter, but recovery efforts for B.E. were stalled by weather until May 12.

Analysis

It is clear that the group had a rope, as one of the party rappelled down to the victim after the accident. What is not clear is why B.E. would choose to approach the crevasse to "check" on it without being roped up. (Source: Dave Stephens, Pam Doyle, Canmore Leader)

FALLING ROCK
British Columbia, Yoho National Park, Lake O'Hara, Abbott Pass

Two climbers were ascending the steep approach gullies to Abbott Pass from Lake O'Hara in Yoho National Park on July 25. They were packing heavy packs, planning a few days climbing from the hut at the pass. At 1730, one of them noticed a football sized rock coming towards them. He shouted a warning, but his partner (40) was not able to move in time. A.P. was struck in the head and killed by rockfall while ascending the last 150 metres to the pass and the hut. The custodian at the hut was able to contact the warden service right away on the emergency phone. The deceased and her partner were evacuated by helicopter later the same day.

Analysis

The victim's helmet was on her pack, but it is unlikely that it would have saved her life given the size of the rockfall and the injuries sustained. Picking protected locations for breaks, moving quickly between safe zones, and traveling during the cold early morning parts of the day are possible mitigating measures. The unfortunate party was witnessed as being tight to the Victoria side of the approach gully. The marked trail (blue squares of paint) is in the middle of the gully at this point. Remaining on the marked trail would likely have been safer as there is considerable threat from falling rock off the side of Mount Victoria. Parties should also communicate with any other parties in the gully at the same time and take care to their safety. (Source: Percy Woods, Yoho National Park Warden Service, Barry Blanchard)

STRANDED, PARTY SEPARATED, WEATHER
British Columbia, Yoho National Park, Lake O'Hara, Mount Biddle

On August 8, a party of six climbers headed to the West Ridge of Mount Biddle, a 5.4 alpine rock route on the Lake O'Hara area of Yoho National Park. Two of the party turned around low on the route when they noticed an approaching storm. The other four continued. There are a series of small rock steps on the route interspersed between loose exposed scrambling. Above the technical pitches, G.D. decided to traverse across the Southwest face and disappeared into storm clouds. The rest of his party assumed he had fallen to his death, but carried on up in spite of the ongoing storm. The three reached the summit around 1530. On descent, two of them were able to down-climb the steep sections in the rain, but one of them could not. The only rope in the party was carried by the climber who had earlier disappeared. So the climber waited on the ridge at around 10,000 feet while the other two went for help. The two reported the incident around 0200. Park wardens responded at first light and spotted the climber. The rescue crew attempted to evacuate him by heli-sling, but had to abort due to clouds. Clearing weather a short time later allowed the heli-sling rescue operation to continue.

Searching for the assumed-dead second climber began on the normal climbing route and fall-lines associated with it. The climber was eventually located 300 feet below the summit on ledges on the opposite side on the east face of Biddle. He had traversed on ledges looking for an overhang to sit out the storm under. One rescuer slung into the climber and he was evacuated to the Elizabeth Parker Hut and his elated friends.

Analysis

The forecast for the day was for a severe storm with lightning. Darkening skies by late morning confirmed the forecast and a heavy rain and lightening storm followed. The decision to carry on when the storm became obvious was questionable. The decision above the technical sections to carry on during the storm after one of the climbers was presumed dead is difficult to comprehend. This is particularly puzzling since none of the three had a rope at that point and they likely knew that getting down the steep sections would get increasingly difficult with the rain. (Source: Percy Woods, Yoho National Park Warden Service)

SLIP ON ROCK OR ICE, UNROPED
British Columbia, Yoho National Park, Mount Dennis, Carlsberg Column

On November 19, two climbers were approaching the base of Carlsberg Column (60 m. II WI5), a waterfall ice climb on Mount Dennis in Yoho National Park. B.R. (32) had started traversing on an exposed ledge that went over to the base of the ice climb. His partner J.D. was a short distance behind him adjusting his boots but had yet to start the traverse. Both climbers had put their helmets and crampons on before starting the traverse. J.D. heard a shout and looked up in time to see his partner slipping off the edge of the ledge and disappearing over a short cliff below. J.D. ran down slope to assist his partner, who had fallen over 35 metres. B.R. was seriously injured and unconscious. His partner stabilized him as best he could and went for help at the Yoho Park Information Centre close by in the town of Field. Park Wardens, Field Ambulance, Banff Ambulance and RCMP all attended the accident scene. B.R. was heli-slung out to an awaiting ambulance and later transferred to STARS air ambulance. He died of his injuries a short time later in hospital. (Source: Percy Woods, Yoho National Park Warden Service)

FALL ON ICE—ICE TOOLS PULLED OUT, UNROPED
Quebec, Mont du Gros Bras

On February 22, J.S. (39) and M.L.(38) had finished the Gros Bras route at Weir and were packing up their gear when they decided to have a look at the rock climbs further along the cliff. On the way back J.S. decided to attempt an unroped mixed traverse across the ice shrouded base of the cliff. After one or two moves, he noticed the ice was very poor and was just beginning to step back down onto level ground when the ice supporting his left tool disintegrated and he fell heavily downward about half a metre, firmly planting his right crampon, unfortunately he also fell backwards on his planted foot and snapped his tibia, just above the boot top, and his fibula near the knee. He then proceeded to flip onto his back, fall about one more metre and luckily landed in between two large boulders which stopped him falling further. J.S. also sustained severe bruising. M.L. quickly came to J.S.'s aid organizing some of the other climbers. Fortunately two of the other climbers present were very experienced and well qualified in first aid and they improvised a splint from slings and a dead sapling, ensured J.S. was warm and not in shock, and, when stabilized, proceeded to move J.S., via a two-man carry with a relay of three persons, to M.L.'s car.

Analysis

Even a short fall when wearing crampons can have serious consequences. (Source: John Scoles)

FALL ON ROCK, UNROPED, CLIMBING ALONE
Quebec, Mont Saint Hilaire

On September 6, a hiker made a macabre discovery at the foot of the northern slopes of Mont Saint Hilaire. A body rested among the rocks at the foot of a 250 metre high cliff near the "Cave of the Fairies." A camera was located by the search and rescue team near Y.L.'s body.

It is surmised that Y.L. was alone and decided to climb the cliff in an attempt to take photographs. It appears that Y.L. (30) ascended in an area which was particularly difficult to climb without proper climbing gear, which he did not have. He lost his footing and fell approximately 50 metres to his death. A local resident thought that he heard a cry at approximately 1930 the night before on September 5, but he did not alert authorities due to the large number of hikers in this popular area. The victim was not immediately identified, as he was not carrying any identification.

Analysis

Parties are often lured into situations where their ambitions exceed their skills and physical abilities. Your best protection is to know your own limits (and those of your partners) and to resist being tempted far beyond them. (Source: Roger LaFrance–L'Oeil Regional, Steve Castonguay)

FALL ON ROCK
Yukon Territory, Kluane National Park Reserve, Mount Logan

A trio of experienced climbers, Stephen Canning (22), and his two partners (36 and 43) registered to climb Mount Logan's East Ridge on May 7. They expected to be done their expedition on June 4. When the trio started their attempt at the East Ridge's summit about noon on May 22, the weather was clear. They crested the East Peak just after midnight. Increasingly stormy weather forced them to camp not far from the summit. At midnight on May 23, they started back down. S.C. was about 15 metres away from one of his partners when he stopped to take a photo—about 0630. His climbing partner looked away briefly, only to look back as the younger man fell off the snowy, rocky face. At the time it was windy and a storm was moving in. Nobody witnessed the actual cause of the fall, but they did witness the fall itself. The fall happened at 5,850 metres, just 100 metres shy of the summit. S.C.'s partners climbed down to him and tried to administer first aid, but S.C. had no vital signs. The surviving pair continued their descent and were forced to camp for two days to wait out inclement weather. Once back at basecamp, the survivors called RCMP on the group's satellite phone, which had been left in camp. Retrieval efforts were unsuccessful, but the two survivors were flown out several days later.

Analysis

Weather and the effects of high altitude are usually factors in incidents like this one. Perhaps the victim was also distracted by his photography. (Source, An article by Sarah Brown in *The Whitehorse Star*, and Jeff Hunston)

(Editor's Note: We learned of a drowning in the Rundle Glacier outwash stream —Owl River, on Baffin Island in Auyuittuq National Park. Del Hildebrand (61) lost his footing and was carried tumbling downstream. He was unable, or just did not, shed his pack. This was not on a mountaineering trip, but worth mentioning because many approaches to big climbs include the need to cross cold, swift streams.

We have also learned that the bodies of the two missing climbers, Daniel Pauze and Susan Barnes, in the Torngat Mountains in northern Labrador last year have been recovered. From notes in the summit register and photos recovered, it appears that the duo successfully climbed to the summit of Mount Caubvick (D'Iberville) in a "wicked snowstorm." Both had inadequate clothing for the conditions. It appears that D.P.'s rappel anchor pulled out and he fell to the base of the Koroc step with the only rope, sustaining leg injuries. His female partner was unable to descend the same route without a rope. Her body was later found on a ledge feature known as the "football field" about a kilometre away from D.P. Both climbers likely perished from exposure.)

UNITED STATES

FALLING SNOW BLOCK
Alaska, Denali National Park, Mount Barrille

A party of four, Dr. Jim Sprott, Niles Woods, Martina Volfova and Kneeland Taylor, flew into the Ruth Glacier on April 19 with Talkeetna Air Taxi. On the 20th the group climbed Mount Dickey and on the 22nd they attempted a different route on Mount Barrille but turned around due to poor snow conditions. Also on the 22nd Taylor flew out of the range leaving a party of three. Two inches of snow fell on Thursday night. Due to weather conditions, the group got a late start on Friday for their attempt on the Japanese Couloir on Barrille. They departed camp about 1000 and began climbing at 1115 following the tracks of a group who had climbed the route the previous day.

After climbing about 700 feet, the group swapped leads and continued climbing. Between 1145 and 1215 while they were ascending, with Volfova leading and Woods in the middle, a picnic table-size chunk of consolidated snow came down from far above and knocked all three climbers down. They slid about 300 feet before a combination of their self-arrest efforts and soft snow stopped their fall.

All acknowledged that they were OK promptly, but Woods immediately complained of pain in his right knee. Dr. Sprott examined Woods and splinted the right leg. After activating their ELT, Sprott and Volfova were able to lower Woods 225 feet to where they felt comfortable traveling without a belay, and were able to holler out to a nearby group. The other group responded with a sled, and they all transported Woods over to a location where TAT had landed.

Woods and Sprott were air transported back to Talkeetna where the Talkeetna Volunteer Rescue Squad transported Woods to the hospital. Woods was diagnosed and treated for a broken right tibia, cracked right pelvis, lacerated liver and bruised kidneys. Volfova was flown back to Talkeetna the next morning.

Analysis

Short of not climbing that route on that day, this was one of those accidents that could be described as an "act of nature." There are hazards in the mountains, and it is impossible to mitigate all of them.

FALLING SNOW
Alaska, Denali National Park, Peak 11,300

Around 0500 on May 3, Mountaineering Ranger Karen Hilton and her two volunteers, Carl Oswald and Matthew Smith, left their camp to patrol the Southwest Ridge of Peak 11,300, located in the West Fork of the Ruth Glacier.

For three days prior to this attempt, warm daytime temperatures and freezing nighttime temperatures provided stable melt-freeze snow conditions on the ridge. Footprints in the snow from an ascent the previous day also allowed for quick route finding through and around the short rock buttresses that characterize the route itself. The team found themselves making good time, reaching approximately 9,600 feet at the top of a major feature called "the S couloir " by 1300. The route brought the team to a traverse on the east side of the ridge where a belay was made about 50-80 feet below the true ridge. It was at this time that a C-130 military aircraft flew over the team twice, causing concern over a possible incident elsewhere in the range. Hilton immediately established communication with the Talkeetna Ranger Station via park radio. The Station confirmed that no incident was occurring. Just seconds after placing the radio back into her pack, Hilton and her team were unexpectedly struck by a large piece of falling ice and snow. Both Oswald and Smith stated they were not hurt. However, Hilton suffered intense pain in her right arm with limited movement. Due to the immediate swelling that occurred, the team climbed an additional 50 feet and rappelled to the nearest bivouac site. After assessing her injuries, Hilton decided it would be ill-advised to continue climbing that day. South District Ranger Daryl Miller was immediately updated of the situation via satellite phone and the Talkeetna Ranger Station by park radio. By morning, Hilton's condition had not significantly changed, and the team chose to retreat.

Hilton and her team descended the south face and arrived back at camp at the base of Peak 11,300 by 1900. The following morning, the team was picked up by Talkeetna Air Taxi and transported to Talkeetna where Hilton received treatment for her injuries.

Analysis

Being at the right place at the wrong time tends to best describe the incident that occurred during this park patrol in the Ruth Glacier area. Unfortunately, the cycle of warm daytime and cold nighttime temperatures that helped provide ideal climbing conditions on this route also caused the release of the snow and ice that forced this team to retreat. The climbing on Peak 11,300 is mainly concentrated on the ridge itself, which mitigates the exposure to objective danger from above. However, this incident is a good reminder of just how quickly the sun can affect even the smallest patches of snow and cause instability.

FALL ON SNOW, RESCUE HAMPERED BY WEATHER
Alaska, Denali National Park, Mount McKinley, West Buttress

The following account is that of a difficult and intense Denali Search and Rescue operation conducted on the upper slopes of Mount McKinley. The individuals who participated in the rescue operation were Renny Jackson, Chris Harder, Steve Rickert, Jack McConnell, and David Bywater. It is also imperative to mention two British climbers who played key roles in the rescue operation and without whom it might not have been accomplished: Andy Perkins and Neil McNabb, who were awarded the "Pro-Pin Award" for the 2004 climbing season.

On May 19, Il Ho Cho (40), a Korean climber, reportedly had taken a 50-60 foot fall somewhere above Denali Pass, 18,200 feet on the West Buttress. Cho and his climbing partner were descending when the fall occurred. Cho was unable to move any farther because of his injuries. His partner descended to the 17,000-foot camp to try to get help. Three different Korean climbing parties who were at 17,000 feet made two separate attempts to get emergency supplies back up to where Cho lay. Both attempts were turned back by high winds and whiteout conditions, One resulted in a significant fall by one of the party members.

Given the fact that Cho had suffered a head injury and had spent the night out in the open with very little equipment, his chances of being alive were at best very slim. Jackson assembled an initial response team consisting of Harder, Rickert, Bywater, and McConnell. They left the 14,200-foot camp about 0600, and Perkins and McNabb followed them about an hour later. The Teton group arrived at the 17,200-foot camp after 3.5 hours of climbing. Jackson directed his team to rehydrate and set up a camp while he attempted to obtain information from the several South Korean climbing groups who were also camped there. Jackson contacted Talkeetna Ranger Station by radio. They set up a relay with a Korean interpreter. After lengthy discussions between the interpreter and various members of the climbing parties, Jackson was able to determine that Cho's position was near Denali Pass. The weather, however, was deteriorating significantly with increasing winds and poor visibility.

After Jackson discussed the situation with Talkeetna, he decided to put together an initial response team of McConnell, Harder, Perkins, McNabb, and himself. Perkins and McNabb began climbing ahead of the others in order to check out the higher route that traversed to Denali Pass and mark a few of the fixed pickets on the traverse as "way points" for our return using a GPS unit. McConnell, Harder, and Jackson followed Perkins and McNabb about 15 minutes later with additional evacuation equipment. McConnell carried it the entire way up. Bywater and Rickert stayed behind at the 17,200-foot camp in order to finish setting up the camp that would prove to be very necessary when the team returned. Once the camp was up, Bywater and Rickert were then to start climbing up to Denali Pass in support of first team efforts.

The five rescuers made the traverse up to Denali Pass over the next few hours. Perkins and McNabb contacted Jackson when they arrived at Denali Pass and said that they believed that they could see a "black object" below on the uppermost portion of the Harper Glacier and requested permission to investigate. Just as Jackson's group arrived at the Pass, he received another very excited radio transmission from Perkins, who indicated that they had found Cho and that he appeared to have a pulse and was breathing. While Jackson was excited by the fact that the patient was alive, this was tempered by the realization of just how difficult it was going to be to evacuate him given the very poor weather conditions and the altitude. Harder began an initial assessment of the patient. Cho had an obvious head injury with a large contusion to the area of his left temple. The rescuers put his legs inside his pack and placed him down on the pads from the inside of Jackson and Harder's packs. The five rescuers then clipped into the sled and began to drag him back up to Denali Pass following the wands that Jackson had placed on the way down.

When they arrived at Denali Pass they were met with the full force of the incoming storm, strong winds and wind-driven snow. Jackson placed the first lowering anchor—an ice ax—stepped on it, clipped in one of their two climbing ropes, and began the first of the many lowerings that we were to do that day. Harder and McConnell acted as litter attendants and traversed over to begin work on the next anchor. Shouting over the wind, Jackson reminded them to move lightly, as we were all on a single ice ax at this point. This leapfrogging method of moving the patient was to be repeated many times over the next several hours. As they down-climbed slowly across, Jackson was aware that the avalanche hazard was increasing. The main problems that plagued the rescuers throughout the day were the poor visibility and whiteout conditions. Many times Jackson was unable to see across the slope to Perkins and McNabb who were in the process of creating the next set of anchors. At some point during the rescue, Rickert and Bywater joined the small group, having come up from 17,200 feet at our request. Bywater was able to replace an exhausted Harder as a litter attendant while Rickert joined Jackson for assistance with anchor construction. The secondary team, having been assembled from climbers at 17,200-foot camp, met up with the main team when they were nearly finished with the main portion of the traverse, which was a great help as well.

The Teton crew (visiting rangers) occupied two tents side by side with Harder and Rickert providing badly needed medical attention to Cho. They were up most of the night with the patient. Clear skies prevailed on Saturday morning, May 21. The Teton crew was in no condition to do much of anything other than continue rehydrating and sleeping throughout much of the day. During the afternoon they rallied and we stomped out a landing zone and prepared Cho for his departure, as best we could. When it appeared that the low-lying clouds had dissipated enough, Talkeetna dispatched the NPS Lama helicopter with pilot Jim Hood towards the mountain. As Hood approached the Kahiltna Glacier, he found that the visibility was not adequate, so he was forced to return to Talkeetna.

For the second time in less than a week, the Teton crew prepared for a 2,500-foot technical lowering of Cho down to the 14,200-foot camp. Rickert attended the patient during the lowering. Two-and-one-half hours after we started, Cho was in the medical tent at 14,200 feet.

This rescue was successful because the many people who were involved, but without the valiant and on-site efforts by the Teton crew, it would have had a different outcome for the Korean climber Cho.

OVERDUE—INADEQUATE COMMUNICATIONS
Alaska, Denali National Park, Mount McKinley, Cassin Ridge

On June 3, Ranger Joe Reichert requested a search for overdue climbers Sue Nott and Karen McNeill of the "Best Chilled" expedition climbing the Cassin Ridge. According to Reichert, the party reported they had five days of food and seven days of fuel when they departed the 14,200-foot camp on May 25. By June 3 they had been out for nine days. At 1131, a tent was spotted on the summit by the NPS Lama helicopter. A subsequent flight confirmed that the two climbers who were camped on the summit were wearing clothing similar to that of Nott and McNeill. The party was confirmed to be Nott and McNeill at 1657 when they arrived at the 17,200-foot camp.

Analysis

This is an example of what is often referred to as "preventive" search and rescue. By using the helicopter for aerial searches, climbing rangers did not need to gather resources for a ground search and expose themselves to harsh weather conditions and technical climbing dangers while not certain about whether or not a serious condition did exist for those that were, in theory, overdue. Rangers were able to locate the climbing party quickly and without putting large numbers of resources into the field. The climbers were aware that they were overdue according to the information that they left with the NPS Rangers, yet made no motion for assistance when they encountered the NPS helicopter.

This search may have been prevented if the team had taken their radio. They could have called either the 14,200-foot camp or the basecamp manager at the 7,200-foot camp and asked them to inform NPS personnel that they were doing well and not in need of any assistance. McNeill later stated that, "… when it came down to packing (for the climb), the antenna was misplaced." The decision to take a radio is a personal one and one that must be weighed by each individual party. As it turned out for McNeill and Nott, this option was eliminated by the misplaced antenna.

The NPS will now take route specific information regarding equipment, number of days of food and fuel, communication equipment and overdue dates at remote duty stations. Climbers who leave this information will be told of the NPS intention to start a search approximately 48 hours after their overdue date, unless there are conditions that may indicate a search is warranted before such time.

Up until now, a team was not officially considered overdue until after the return date given to the Rangers at the Talkeetna Ranger Station. This has proven to be a problem for those parties climbing multiple routes over the course of many weeks. NPS Rangers have taken informal itineraries over the years, but this incident highlighted the need for formal recording of itineraries and due dates for short climbs that are to be completed before the official return date left in Talkeetna. Climbers must also be advised that they will be considered overdue approximately 48 hours after the return date given to the Ranger at the remote location and that they need to remember to notify the Ranger upon their return to camp.

AMS
Alaska, Denali National Park, Mount McKinley, West Buttress
On the evening of June 6, the Russian Denali Expedition requested the assistance of the NPS volunteer doctor at the 17,200-foot camp on the West Buttress of Mount McKinley because one member of the team was ill. Upon investigation, Dr. McLean discovered Ludmila Korobeshko (29) sick with acute mountain sickness and possibly high altitude pulmonary edema. Reichert and McLean escorted Korobeshko down to the 14,200-foot ranger camp where she remained on oxygen for 30 hours before descending with her team to basecamp.

Analysis
During and interview with Dr. McLean, Korobeshko stated that she had had a persistent headache during her two days at 14,200-foot camp. In hindsight it appears that Korobeshko had acute mountain sickness beginning at this camp. Climbers need to be honest with themselves and their partners with regards to their health. Korobeshko should have rested at the 14,200-foot camp until she felt 100 percent.

The National Park Service recommends a time line for ascending the West Buttress that provides most climbers adequate acclimatization. The prescribed time is ten to 13 days up to the high camp at 17,200 feet. The Russian team moved to this camp on their 9th day on the mountain and climbed to the summit on their 9th day. It is fortunate that more of the team did not get seriously ill.

Every year there are some who will push themselves to climb Mount McKinley as fast as they can. While some succeed without event, the consequence of becoming sick high on the mountain can be fatal.

DEEP-VEIN THROMBOSIS—INADEQUATE MEDICATION SUPPLY
Alaska, Denali National Park, Mount McKinley, West Buttress
On June 6, Anatoli Lakteonov of the same Russian team as above was brought by members of his expedition to the NPS Basecamp. Patient was

observed to be visibly limping and in some distress. Examination of the patient's right leg revealed minimum one-inch pitting edema distal to the knee, extending to mid-shaft tibia. Patient also had wrapped his leg with ace wrap from the groin to just below his knee. Pain was reported upon palpation to mid-femoral region. Also felt was a hard cord-like structure within the right medial femoral area. Diagnosis made was a suspected DVT (deep vein thrombosis) of the great saphenous vein. Dr. Dickey (Alaska Regional Hospital ER) was consulted and he agreed with the diagnosis and with the recommendation of immediate evacuation. These findings were reported to the IC at Talkeetna (Ranger Roger Robinson). Attempts were made to use a helicopter from the Alaska Air National Guard rescue unit, but Talkeetna Air Taxi ultimately carried out the evacuation. Patient was *not* medically escorted during the flight out, as it was determined that weather conditions would be unduly hazardous. Patient was met at the Talkeetna airport by NPS personnel and then transferred to a Life Guard helicopter for final transport to Providence Hospital in Anchorage, AK. Patient was definitively diagnosed as having a DVT and was admitted for treatment.

Analysis

The patient had a previous medical history of DVTs and pulmonary embolisms. During the climb, he was taking prescribed blood thinners, but did not have a supply adequate for the duration of the climb.

ILLNESS, FAILURE TO DISCLOSE PREVIOUS MEDICAL HISTORY, INEXPERIENCE
Alaska, Denali National Park, Mount McKinley, West Buttress

On June 12, Tina James, a client with Mountain Trip led by Todd Ruthledge, was out on a summit bid when she began experiencing medical problems. The group had left high camp around 0930 and had reached Denali Pass around noon. James had been moving very slowly. When queried, she said she was having difficulty breathing and had a headache. She claimed not to be dizzy or nauseated and was not exhibiting any ataxia according to Ruthledge. He also discovered at this time from James' friends on the trip that she seemed to be suffering from a chest cold and had taken an antibiotic, amoxicillin, though the previous evening she was not experiencing a cough. Ruthledge did not feel James was exhibiting any severe signs of Acute Mountain Sickness (AMS) and decided to send her down with assistant guide Drew Ludwig while he and the rest of the group continued to the summit. Ludwig and James began their descent back to high camp. En route James may have lost consciousness briefly and had to be physically helped the remainder of the way into camp. They arrived in camp at 1515 and immediately contacted the NPS. Ranger Meg Perdue and VIP Ranger Darren Castell were at high camp and responded performing an initial assessment of James, whose chief complaints were severe headache, difficulty breathing, and chest pain. James described the pain as "crushing" and said that it was radiating down her left arm. She said she had no cardiac history but had had surgery five weeks earlier for a severed artery in her left forearm. Perdue later determined that James had not shared this fact with Ruthledge along with the information about taking antibiotics and taking meperidine for a toothache. James was placed on oxygen and allowed to rest in her tent while Perdue conferred with staff at the 14,200-foot camp. By 1600, James stated that the chest pain was gone and her breathing was improved with the supplemental oxygen, but she still had a severe headache. Though her condition had improved somewhat, due to the uncertainty and potential instability of James' condition, the decision was made to attempt a ground evacuation from 17,200 feet. Gusting wind conditions prevented an air evacuation. After resting, James felt she could walk down rather than needing to be lowered. The decision was made to descend the ridge to 16,200 feet with Perdue short-roping James.

James was at 14,200 feet by 2135 and undergoing an assessment by staff there. She remained on oxygen and was kept overnight. Her condition was deemed stable and so James was released the following morning at 1000 to descend with her party to basecamp. According to Todd Ruthledge, the descent from 14,200 feet to 11,200 feet on June 13, was slow but steady; however, because the team had gone from 17,200 feet that day. James was exhausted so she decided to camp at 11,200 feet. On June 14 they continued their descent, though James' headache had returned and she appeared weak. They met with Ranger Gordy Kito's patrol at 7,800 feet. James was reassessed and advised to continue to descend. The group reached basecamp at 1600 and was able to fly out almost immediately. Upon returning to Talkeetna James called her mother, who reminded her she is allergic to penicillin. Amoxicillin is in that same family of antibiotics.

Analysis

Here is another classic example of the importance of and need for good communication among expedition members, particularly between clients and guides. It also illustrates the equally important principle of not placing ambitions for the summit ahead of good judgment. If she had been willing to discuss her medical conditions and concerns with her guides, it may have been possible to avoid the situation she found herself in or at least lessen its seriousness. It is unknown whether there was more than an allergic reaction contributing to James medical problems, but it is clear that with so many conditions affecting her, respiratory problems of unknown etiology, a toothache, and major surgery within the past several weeks, a more conservative approach and willingness to place personal well-being ahead of the summit would have been prudent.

POOR EXPEDITION BEHAVIOR–PARTY SEPARATED (ABANDONED IN-JURED AND ILL TEAMMATES), INADEQUATE MAINTENANCE OF TENTS DURING STORM, FAILURE TO FOLLOW DIRECTIONS

Alaska, Denali National Park, Mount McKinley, West Buttress

On June 13, Ranger Meg Perdue received a radio call from VIP (Volunteer in Parks) Dave Hughes regarding a climber he had just contacted who had injured his ankle and been left alone by his party. Hughes and another VIP, Darren Castill, were returning to the 17,200-foot high camp with oxygen bottles they had retrieved from a cache at 16,200-feet when they met with Tomasz Pyjor of the seven man "Annapurna Klub" expedition below Washburn's Thumb around 16,600 feet. Pyjor had injured his ankle and was awaiting assistance to continue to high camp. Three of his team had moved up the previous day and the remaining three, with whom he had been traveling, had continued on to high camp in hopes of finding the others to assist Pyjor. Perdue then contacted two members of the group, the expedition leader, Robert Rozmus, and Marcin Kuras at high camp. Perdue questioned them about the circumstances around leaving Pyjor, and in the course of discussions, realized that they had left a second member, Lech Slawski, who was sick and moving slowly, alone above Washburn's Thumb near 16,900 feet.

Rozmus stated that they had come ahead to find the other three members of the group and wanted to bring Pyjor and Slawski to high camp despite the fact that one was injured and the other sick. The group of three, who had ascended to high camp the previous day, were nowhere in high camp. It was later determined they were still out on a summit bid at that time. Perdue informed Rozmus that it was inappropriate and unsafe to leave teammates alone, particularly when sick and injured, and that their intention to find assistance to help them continue up to high camp was absolutely ill-advised. Perdue strongly recommended that Rozmus and Kuras descend to assist their teammates and continue descending back to the 14,200-foot camp, as it was clear that individually and as a team they were ill-prepared to deal appropriately with conditions. Rozmus refused, stating that there was "no problem" and they would take care of the situation. Perdue then warned Rozmus that if their group required further assistance caused by incompetence on their part, they would be cited for Creating a Hazardous Condition (36 CFR 2.34 (a)(4) Disorderly Conduct). Rozmus acknowledged that he understood.

On the following day Perdue recontacted the group as the three members who had summited the previous day, Andrzej Michalczewski, Roman Dzida, Michal Wyganowski, and the injured member, Tomasz Pyjor, were preparing to descend. Apparently, this part of the group, rather than wait for the rest of their team at 14,200 feet, descended all the way to basecamp and flew out around June 15. The three remaining members, Rozmus, Kuras, and the sick member Slawski, planned to stay and still attempt a summit bid. Perdue again reiterated the need for the group to stay together and be responsible for one another, take conditions seriously, and act appropriately. All three nodded agreement to this.

In the ensuing days a storm enveloped high camp resulting in people's inability to do anything more than get out and shovel out their tents and reinforce snow walls. At the height of the storm, with winds in excess of 80 mph, several groups had their tents destroyed and either built snow caves, moved in with other groups or asked for assistance (tent space) from the NPS. It should also be noted that many other groups and tents survived the storm. Those groups were the ones with the best snow walls whose members actively worked to maintain them.

On the evening of June 17 at 2015 as the storm was abating, Rozmus came to the NPS tent and requested a tent, stating that the group's two tents, both North Face VE25s, had been destroyed. Incidentally, this was the same type of tent used by the NPS which survived the very same storm. Perdue went to retrieve a tent from the rescue cache for the group. Upon reaching the cache she found the door ajar and many items, including all of the ropes used for technical rescues, strewn about. The bags in which the ropes were contained were packed full of wind-transported snow and were frozen and thus useless in their present condition. It was also impossible to know if any items had been lost due to the winds. Perdue found Kuras and Slawski inside the cache container itself. When asked why they did not take one of the tents from the cache, which were in plain view, or dig a snow cave rather than jeopardize the cache and its contents, Rozmus offered no other explanation than it was "too difficult." The group was incapable of setting the tent up on their own so Perdue and VIP Michael Dong had to assist them. Further, the team would not make the necessary efforts to build walls around the tent to protect it from the still-strong winds. As a result, the NPS tent was damaged overnight.

On the morning of June 18 the winds abated enough that it was possible to consider descending. Perdue went to each party at high camp to give weather information and find out their intentions. All the groups at high camp except for one were already in the process of packing up and planning to descend. At 1030, Perdue went to the tent given to the Annapurna members to use. It was clear to Perdue from her interaction with them and their utter lack of self-motivation and inability to grasp the gravity of their situation that they must be made to move down while they still had a chance of doing so under their own power. Perdue informed them they must go down. After they refused by making no move to pack up, Perdue began to take down the tent. They finally and extremely begrudgingly began to move and Perdue was forced to stay and assist and watch over the entire process. The group finally began their descent around 1300.

Perdue and Dong waited for all parties to depart high camp and did some clean up and reorganization of the cache prior to beginning their descent at 1830. Perdue and Dong assisted in a lowering from the base of the head wall during their descent and still managed to make it to the 14,200-foot camp within an hour of the Annapurna expedition. Again, at 14,200 feet, the Annapurna group requested a tent and required assistance from NPS staff to set it up. During this time the patient who had been lowered to 14,200 feet was evacuated via Lama helicopter, at which point Slawskie stated that he wanted a helicopter evacuation and claimed to have insurance that could cover it. He was informed that evacuation decisions were strictly based on need, not personal desires.

The group left to descend to basecamp the following day. It was only discovered after their departure that they had left a full gallon of fuel in the Ranger camp. They arrived at basecamp sometime that night and were discovered the following morning by the basecamp ranger, Karen Hilton, to be sleeping in the fuel tent.

Analysis

From start to finish, this expedition showed a total disregard for their own safety and others. Their unwillingness to put aside their personal goals in light of their clear inability to deal appropriately under adverse conditions indicates that the only way to impress upon them the seriousness of their negligence was to issue them citations for Disorderly Conduct and Tampering. Hopefully, this will send a clear message that such behavior by anyone will not be tolerated.

FALLING ROCK
Alaska, Denali National Park, Mount McKinley, West Buttress

The Alaska Mountaineering School (AMS)-8 expedition led by Rob Gowler flew to basecamp on the southeast fork of the Kahiltna Glacier on June 10. The group progressed steadily up the West Buttress route. Even with several long delays due to weather, the entire team reached the summit on June 26. On the 27th they departed high camp planning to descend to basecamp. They spent a six hours at the 14,200-foot camp and continued their descent at 2110 in three roped teams of four with a guide at the rear of each team.

At 2140, as the first roped team was rounding the toe of Windy Corner, they heard a loud crack and an enormous quantity of rocks came cascading down, striking the first three climbers on the first rope team. Guide Steve Grillo was the fourth person on that roped team and felt a strong tug on the rope as he was on the ground in self-arrest position. Once the rocks stopped falling the first three people on the rope, Mark Morford, Gerb Islei, and Clint West were all seriously injured. Gowler witnessed the event and immediately started calling for help on his cell phone. His initial attempts to call the 14,200-foot and 7,200-foot ranger camps were not answered, so he called the basecamp manager who notified ranger John Evans and then called AMS head quarters in Talkeetna to alert people that he had three serious injuries and needed a helicopter as soon as possible.

By 2205, rescue personnel at 14,200-foot camp, at basecamp and in Talkeetna were all mobilized for the rescue effort. Ranger Joe Reichert was incident commander. By 2311 the Park Service contract rescue helicopter (Lama) and a twin engine Navajo piloted by Erik Dinklewater of Talkeetna Aero were both in the air headed toward Windy Corner.

At 2326, a patient update was transmitted from para-rescue man David Shuman to the 14,200-foot camp. One person, Clint West (47) was deceased, Mark Morford (47) had a femur and wrist fracture and Gerd Islei (56) had several broken ribs, a collapsed lung, and a ruptured disc in his lower back.

An air rescue evacuation ensued.

Analysis

While traveling in mountainous terrain has certain inherent risks, the rockfall danger on the West Buttress route has never been a significant concern. This team was in a position that many are in during the course of the climbing season. They were traveling at night, when cooler temperatures and frozen conditions make it safer to travel. They were very unlucky. No other known fatalities have occurred due to rock-fall on Mount McKinley. We all hope that rock-fall in the Windy Corner area does not become more common. (Source: All Denali accounts are edited from reports written by various Denali National Park South District Rangers)

(Editor's Note: There were a few other incidents on Mount McKinley and one in Wrangell-St. Elias National Park during the climbing season. Two were medical problems—an acute abdomen and a case of HAPE—and one psychological problem, in which a client was threatening to harm himself and others in the group. When the parents of that person were contacted, they did not express any surprise.

There was one plane incident on the Ruth Glacier—a crash on take off. There were no injuries.

On May 4, Jason Harper, c. 28, was dropped off at Windy Ridge for an attempt on Mount Sanford. When the pilot returned to pick him up on May 9, he was nowhere to be found. After 12 days of searching and finding no trace, the presumption is that he perished.

On June 27, the body of Thomas Gary Cole was discovered at a cache site at the 17,200-foot level. An examination of the records indicated that he died June 19, 1969, of pulmonary edema at this camp. On July 1, his body was reburied at the 14,200-foot level.

There are approximately 34 other climbers that have not been recovered from the slopes of Denali. Depending on the location, other climbers may or may not have the misfortune of coming across these remains. Bodies that are found in remote areas should not be disturbed until professionals can get to the scene to determine who the victim was and preserve any evidence around the site.

This was a very unfortunate discovery for all of those involved. We are pleased to have left Mr. Cole's body in a location of his choosing, and that in the end one of his last requests, to remain on the slopes of Mount McKinley, was granted.)

FALL ON ROCK—ATTACKED BY BEES
Arizona, Camelback Mountain, Hart Route

Dear Climbing Community: My name is Jeff, and I am the climber who survived this incident. I want to try to clear up what happened to let all the climbers in the area know what to be wary of and where. I have been climbing for over ten years, but I live in Michigan, which is devoid of outdoor areas, and only get outdoors about once a year. This was Keith's first time climbing outside. That is why we were doing an easy route, listed at 5.2 in the Phoenix area *Climbers Guide*.

We had reached the belay at the top of the third pitch and were having a great time when the bees hit, just a few at first, and then suddenly they swarmed us. As we were trying to decide to go up or down, I looked up and saw what I believe to be the nest about ten feet above us and to the left. Seeing them above us, I decided we were best to go down. By this time they were hitting us very hard and it became difficult to see or even breathe, as they would fly into my mouth every time I opened it to take a breath. All this was compounded by the fact that I AM allergic to bees; however, as stated in other entries some people are only allergic to certain varieties of bees, and I am one of those people. Being from Michigan and having no prior exposure to the bees of the area, let alone the Africanized bees, I feared for my life and knew we had to get down as fast as possible.

At the time we were in the middle of changing over gear to do the last pitch and had the anchor in and were clipped to it but the rope was in a pile to be back-fed for the next pitch. I sent Keith down to the last ledge as I lowered him hand over hand to it. When he has safely reached it I slapped the rope into the anchor, thinking it would at least be a failsafe as we descended, as I did not feel I had time or the ability to set up a rappel with the bees now stinging my eyes. We down-climbed to about halfway between the first and second pitch when we ran out of rope, either from being at the end or from the rope tangling as we descended. I do not know. At this point we were only twenty feet above the belay ledge and up only seventy feet or so. Feeling we were in serious danger from the bees and on easy climbing, I told Keith that we would have to untie and down-climb the rest of the way and he agreed. We untied and I told Keith to go and I would be right behind him. He only made it about ten feet before he fell. He hit the belay ledge and rolled/bounced off and disappeared out of my sight.

I down-climbed the rest or the way and began blindly running around trying to get the bees off and find Keith at the same time. I never found him because shortly after I hit the ground, witnesses grabbed me and drug me up the hill toward the monk to escape the bees. I pointed as best I could in the direction I thought Keith lay. Half the group ran that way, the other half got me out of the area.

Analysis

No prior incident of swarm attack has been reported previously on this route, but there have been reports of bees attacking climbers on Camelback Mountain, one of which, in 2001, resulted in a fall causing broken vertebrae. That hive has since been destroyed.

Note that a prescription epi-pen is also a good item to put in one's first aid kit, whether you are allergic to bees or not. (Some people don't know if they are or not because they have never been stung.) These are available from most pharmacies and a family doctor can prescribe them.

Experts have suggested assuming that all bees in Arizona are "African-ized"—aggressive and will attack in a swarm and potentially pursue. Bees' life-cycle makes them particularly aggressive during early spring when the air temperature increases and desert flowers begin to bloom. In particular, this is when the queen may be found outside of the hive. If this is the case the workers will be particularly aggressive in their defense of the queen. All stinging insects should be ignored and not swatted because in some species, injury to one insect causes a pheromone to be released that attracts the others and causes them to attack. Common advice is to let the insects land on you, and even sting you, rather than swat or kill them and provoke a swarm attack. This of course is easier said than done, and particularly so for someone with allergies.

Regarding the team's escape once the bee attack had begun, the rope set up to rappel was doubled over, in a classic setup to pull down. Had the rope been tied only at one end, it should have reached all the way to the ground if not tangled. In addition, unbeknownst to the climbers, there is a lesser known gully directly below the route they were climbing which would have allowed them a more direct escape than trying to rappel/climb back down the original route itself. Both these facts would have been difficult to assimilate during the attack.

Finally, the fall victim was *not* wearing a helmet and suffered head injuries that may have been reduced if he had been. Given the height of the fall, however, the effect this had on the final result is unclear. (Source: From a letter from Jeff, with some edits, and from a report compiled by Bob Zimer-ing, Rescue Technician I, Maricopa County Sheriff's Office, part of Central Arizona Mountain Rescue Association)

RAPPEL FAILURE–ACCIDENTAL MANUAL DISENGAGEMENT OF ASCENT DEVICE, INADEQUATE EQUIPMENT, CLIMBING ALONE, NO HARD HAT
Arizona, Phoenix, Saguaro

On April 29, I (Jeff Gertsch, 26) was out in the middle of the desert at my climbing spot alone, ascending a fixed rope for the purpose of bolting a sport climbing route using a single Wild Country Ropeman. After ascent to the drill site at 20+ feet, I needed to drop down a foot to hammer the bolt, opened the manual disengage on the ascender, and descended fine, locked up the teeth on the ascender again. However, in reaching for the hammer, I did not realize my finger was still slightly in the disengage cord, and by the motion of reaching for the hammer, unloaded the teeth on the Ropeman (difficult to describe—sort of when you reach out to one side your other arm tends to reach the other way for stability), and began to fall—instantly realized what was happening and pulled my hand away, but I believe the teeth were tardy in grabbing the rope since I was using my new ice climbing rope (fairly slick). I awoke in my harness near the ground.

The ascender did catch and thus I had a rapid deceleration injury with some impact on the ground (not a free fall, however). I had a head injury and loss of consciousness, but released the harness and used a cell phone to call my spouse. She called 911 after I tried to stand but could not. Search and rescue was called and I was life-flighted from the scene.

I spent five days in the intensive care unit and ended up with seven vertebral transverse process fractures, a right pneumo/hemothorax, a fractured rib, an acromioclavicular separation grade II, and a head laceration with concussion and loss of consciousness. Lucky!!!

Analysis

The biggest issue that would have prevented this was the use of a backup ascender, which I normally always do, but (swear to god) one of few times I had ever gotten lazy enough not to throw on another backup ascender, and so I paid for it. Other key issues, however, were not climbing with another person (I was alone on a day off and no friends were around) and not wearing a climbing helmet—especially as I was alone. (Source: Edited from a report written by Jeff Gertsch)

RAPPEL FAILURE—TRYING TO PASS KNOT, CLIMBING ALONE
Arizona, Phoenix, Waterfall Area, White Tank Regional Park

On October 4, Maricopa County Sheriff's Office Mountain Rescue was notified via SAR Coordinator, Deputy Tony Navarra, that a climber had apparently been rappelling and had fallen to his death. Mountain Rescue Units were notified by David Bremson, via Team pager, of the situation so that following Team members would respond appropriately. Mountain Rescue was informed that, according to the climber's family, he had gone rappelling alone and had not returned home the evening of October 3rd.

Analysis

David Bremson noted the following about the climber:
- He had become separated from his harness, which was approximately 175 feet above the subject's location and approximately 100 feet below the top of the cliff.
- His rope did not extend to the ground.

- Two ropes were connected together (red rope anchored to the top of the cliff, white rope tied to red).
- He had, apparently, fallen onto two small ledges prior to coming to rest in an eight-foot high bush growing in the ground.
- His body displayed severe trauma to multiple areas and did not appear to have survived the fall.

The following conclusions were drawn. Due to the configuration of the equipment on the rope, it appears that the man was rappelling down the red rope, reached the knot with the intent of passing it in order to continue rappelling to the ground. There did not appear to be any indication that there were equipment malfunctions. Carabiners were properly locked and an ascender was being used as a back-up device. There did not appear to be any indication that the subject did not double back his harness. Possibly he was unable to properly pass the knot on rappel and may have removed the harness and attempted to move to a ledge and off the cliff.

From information gathered from his wife, A.M. was an experienced climber and rappeller. His equipment seemed to be well worn, suggesting that it was often used. A.M. did leave his wife with information regarding his destination, but since he was alone, he would have been unable to seek immediate assistance in the event that he was able to do so, which he was not in this instance. (Source: From a report submitted by David Bremson, Rescue Specialist with the Maricopa County Sheriff's Office, part of Central Arizona Mountain Rescue Association.)

VARIOUS FALLS ON SNOW ON DESCENT
California, Mount Shasta, Avalanche Gulch

At least ten or twelve people slipped on snow descending Avalanche Gulch on Mount Shasta. Most appear to have been inexperienced. For example, one woman was carrying her ice ax upside down, so when she fell, the pick actually penetrated her neck and trachea! Most falls resulted in fractures or dislocations. These incidents happening on descent account for over 30 percent of this year's number in that category.

There was one fatality in March. A young man (21) climbing with his brother on the Casaval Ridge route was close to the 12,000 foot level when he tripped and fell 1,000 feet. He could not self-arrest. This route is not classified as technical climbing but is very exposed and long falls occur almost yearly, according to the rangers. (Source: From reports submitted by Matt Hill, Lead Climbing Ranger and Eric White, Climbing Ranger)

FALL ON WET ROCK, INADEQUATE PROTECTION,INADEQUATE CLOTHING AND EQUIPMENT, INEXPERIENCE, EXPOSURE, NO HARD HAT
California, Yosemite Valley, Royal Arches

On March 7, Greg McFalls (28) and I, Joe Hardy (25), set out to climb

Royal Arches (III 5.7). It would be the first traditional route we had attempted on our own.

I had been gym, sport, and traditional climbing pretty intensively for a couple of years and could lead 5.11 sport. However, I had led only one trad pitch so I was eager for more. Greg's experience and ability were similar to mine, but he had not led any trad and I was a stronger climber at that point, so we planned that I would do all the leading.

Friends had recommended Royal Arches as a great route, well within our abilities, though with 15-16 pitches we would have to move right along. After doing lots of research about the climb, we picked the month of March because there would be no other parties to slow us down. We knew it would be wet in winter but were told that it wouldn't be a problem. We drove up from the coast early that morning and parked at the Ahwahnee Hotel at 9 a.m. It was still really cold, so we took our time packing and hiked to the climb an hour later.

We had one 60-meter rope, plenty of hardware, lots of food and water, and two FRS (family band) radios for communicating with each other on the pitches. We didn't want extra gear weighing us down and we planned to be down before dark, so we left lights and overnight clothing behind. We also decided not to bring helmets because we thought, "It's a 5.7, it's going to be easy, and there's no one above to drop rocks on us."

The first pitch wasn't hard, but we got a little behind because we had to haul our pack up the chimney and the holds were wet and slimy. We figured the next 400 feet up the ramps would go fast, but a stream pouring down those pitches forced us to the right onto more difficult terrain. By the time we reached the top of the ramps we'd lost our only copy of the topo. I got off route twice trying to find pitch 5, climbing up and down cracks much harder than they were supposed to be until we finally found the right one. By then it was noon and we'd wasted a lot of time.

We knew it was late and we discussed retreating, but the next several pitches promised to be easy, so we decided to give it a shot. We flew up those pitches, finishing the pendulum on pitch 9 a little after 3 p.m. At that point we had three hours of daylight left for six pitches, 16 single-rope rappels, and some third-class down-climbing, all with no topo. But we were optimistic.

Pitch 10 was a 100-foot traverse. It should have been really easy, but the snow on the rim was melting fast in the sun, forcing us to climb across a 40-foot wide cascade. I had to place pro under water in cracks I couldn't see, and by the time we finished the pitch, we were soaked. Pitch 11 was a layback up a big corner. It would be moderate climbing in dry conditions, but the rock was slimy. I was ten feet above my last protection—a sling around a one-inch diameter root when I fell. The root broke and I tumbled about 40 feet. I was shaken mentally, and I'm still surprised that I only suffered a few scrapes and bruises, but I was able to finish the pitch. At that point we felt retreat was out of the question because there was no bolt route down from this location, and with only one rope we would have to leave a lot of gear.

Just as I reached the top of the slimy pitch, two climbers caught up to Greg at the belay below me. They were simul-climbing [climbing simultaneously with protection between them but without an anchored belayer] and moving fast. They asked if they could pass and we agreed. They returned our topo, which they had found on pitch 2, but I had no idea where to go next and I asked them for directions. They offered advice; however, the next pitches were out of sight around a corner and difficult to describe, so I brought Greg up quickly and followed them. They directed me once or twice after that, but then I lost sight of them for just a minute. When I saw them again, they had finished traversing to the left across a slab above me.

Greg and I got to the traverse at about 5:30 p.m. Maybe 45 minutes of daylight remained and the sun was very low. The other party was still in sight and they pointed out the rap route to us. It was only 300 feet above us on easy terrain, so we figured we had it in the bag. Then they climbed out of view and we turned our attention to the traverse. It was supposed to be 5.4, but all I could see was a very smooth 30-foot wide slab a lot harder than that, with nothing for our hands and no protection. In retrospect I think we had climbed too high—we were in a hurry and just didn't explore enough. The simul-climbers had probably assumed we'd have no problem with it, but instead it was the scariest part of the whole climb for me. My shoes were still wet, I was fatigued after so many pitches, and I was facing a long pendulum fall. I made it across after a few tense moments and anchored myself to a tree.

Now it was Greg's turn. Whether it was his wet shoes or a matter of experience, the moves seemed too hard for him so he looked for alternatives. I was pressuring him: "Come on, Greg, you gotta find a way across because it's getting dark and I don't want to be on the cliff tonight." It was dusk now and I probably suspected that a bivy was unavoidable, but we were rushing nevertheless.

A thin, horizontal crack ten feet above us offered Greg some holds. It disappeared halfway across the slab, leaving at least 15 feet of an even steeper face, but he decided to try it anyway. I moved my anchor another 10-15 feet up the cliff—as far as I could go, but as he left the crack, he was still 15-20 feet to the right and five feet above me. He knew he was risking a pendulum fall and he was looking a little uneasy.

There was no warning like, "Joe, I'm going to fall." He just suddenly yelled and I saw him tumbling down the slab in a fetal position. As the rope came tight he swung across the face about 20 feet below me, moving fast. There was no protection between us to shorten the swing. He was facing right—away from me—and swinging left, and the back of his head slammed into a granite block.

He went limp immediately. I thought he'd died. I sat there screaming at him for 30 seconds. Finally I lowered him a few feet until his body draped over a tree trunk. He was still not responding to my calls, so I tied him off and scrambled down some easy 4th-class to where he lay. Within about three minutes of the fall, he started to regain consciousness. Eventually he could answer simple questions, but he was very confused. He had a bloody laceration on his scalp and I was worried about a broken neck, but he was moving OK, he denied any broken bones, and it didn't look like he'd bleed to death. With me pulling on the rope he managed to stumble onto a nearby ledge and lie down. He kept repeating the same comments every five minutes: "Where are we? What happened? I'm sorry, man!" His whole nervous system was affected. His eyes looked funny, his balance was off, and he was sick to his stomach.

It was dusk now. We were 1,300 feet up a 1,500-foot climb and I had to think about what to do. I could go for help, but we had no lights and now I had no belayer. I would just find myself stranded somewhere else. Even if I made it, Greg might become delirious and untie himself before help arrived. If I spent the night with him, we both might freeze to death, but I decided to stay. I never tried to yell for help, because the Valley seemed so far away.

It got chilly right away. I had my fleece pullover and Greg put on his sweatshirt. I laid my water bladder under his head, gave him my long-sleeve shirt for a hat, and as it got colder I took off my fleece and laid it over him. It was probably just above freezing, and we were still wet from traversing the cascade. Sitting there in a T-shirt and light pants and with nothing for my head, hands, or feet, I was the coldest I've ever been for such a long duration. Greg slept some, but I was awake all night. I alternated between lying half on top of him to keep both of us warmer and sitting up moving my arms and rubbing my legs. The wind was gentle and intermittent but felt really cold when it came.

I was desperate for more heat. The moon finally came up about 2 a.m., giving me enough light to find my knife. I cut my fleece down the side, making a small blanket that covered both our torsos. This helped considerably, and I alternated covering my torso and my head to stay sane. By now I couldn't feel my calves and feet and my muscles were so sore from shivering that I was worried we wouldn't be able to function in the morning. Greg occasionally woke up to ask me the same series of confused questions, but I think his head injury helped him sleep. I checked my watch every five minutes.

Dawn came at 6 a.m. At first I couldn't stand up because my legs and feet didn't respond, but I was able to exercise enough to warm up. I got Greg up when the sun finally hit us at 9 a.m. He immediately puked and felt much better after that, although he was still dizzy and a little off balance. It was hard for him to concentrate because his head was throbbing and ringing. Nevertheless, it seemed like he might be able to climb, and the sun was warming us up quickly.

The final pitch was easy, but out of concern for Greg I set an anchor every 30 feet. I watched him closely, keeping tension as he came up, then I climbed again. We made slow but secure progress that way and reached the rap station sometime before noon. Greg was still not totally coherent, but he retained a lot more information now. I had the option of leaving him there and rappelling for help, but he said, "We've been up here long enough. Let's get down." I went over the rigging steps with him several times, "First you get on the rope, then you unclip from the anchor…," and made him repeat everything back to me. When I was satisfied, we started down. I went first so that if he slipped while rappelling I could pull on the rope to control his descent, and I called up to him with the FRS radio to verify that he was rigging the rappel safely.

Now, of course, we were sweating in the sun and we ran out of water halfway down. We didn't get lost, but on one rappel we forgot to remove the knot from one end of the rope and it jammed in the anchor 100 feet above. We pulled and pulled. I was about to try climbing a really thin crack up to the anchor when Greg pulled one more time and got it. That was the last problem we encountered. Greg was much better now and rappelled competently. The descent took about three hours. We were down by 2 p.m.

Prior to the climb I had told my dad that I would call when we got down, but of course I hadn't, so he contacted the park service. A ranger came up to Greg while we were at the hotel parking lot and said, "Are you Joe or Greg, the overdue climbers?" Greg confirmed our identities, but then he mentioned his fall and that he couldn't remember much of the climb. That raised a red flag in the ranger's mind, so he suggested Greg go to the Yosemite clinic. Greg was reluctant, but at that moment he got dizzy, sat down, and puked again. That did it. The ranger called the ambulance and Greg was helicoptered to Fresno for a CAT scan and overnight observation. There was some brain swelling but no fractures or intracranial bleeds, and after a few days of feeling a little groggy, he was fine. Today he remembers starting the climb and everything after he woke up on the ledge, but the accident and most of the pitches before it are simply not there.

Analysis

You may have been chuckling as you read Joe's account, but did you recognize yourself somewhere along the way? Epics due to inexperience are common on easy and moderate multi-pitch routes—see any issue of ANAM (including Tenaya Peak in this issue). When you recommend routes to your neophyte friends, please consider more than just their climbing skill. And give them this article to study. Most of the lessons are obvious, but here is a summary of the key points.

Climbing, protecting, route finding, retreating, forced bivouacs, and dealing with medical emergencies are related but separate skills. Sport climbing won't teach you what you need to know. A new leader and a non-leader make a weak team, especially if the leader becomes incapacitated, so gain experience on shorter traditional climbs where problems can be handled more easily.

Look over the route and the descent before you climb and take a topo for each person. Start a long, unfamiliar route early and allow time for route-finding and descending.

Cold bivouacks are serious business. One underdressed climber died of hypothermia in the park several years ago, in a bivy similar to Joe's and Greg's. Minimum clothing includes balaclavas, warm gloves, and wind/rain shells, in addition to warm tops and bottoms appropriate to the season. If you don't want to sit on a ledge all night, take lights with enough range and staying power to assist with climbing and rappelling.

Don't depend on finding a bolted descent everywhere (or anywhere) on a route. Joe and Greg felt they had passed the point of no retreat at pitch 11, but they could have rappelled from any pitch on the route. Having only one rope, however, would slow them down considerably and force them to leave more gear. On some routes the only anchor options may be a full rope-length apart unless you bring a bolt kit. If you don't trust your injured partner to rappel independently as Greg did, then rappel together. There are several ways to do this.

Learn to recognize when your mental state and/or a string of seemingly minor events are setting you up for an accident. This is one aspect of Situational Awareness—taught to emergency workers, pilots, the military, etc., and it can be a lifesaver. Haste is a common example: Joe and Greg were rushing at the end, psychologically dependent on the other party, and stressed by the lack of time to find the 5.4 traverse. This biased their decisions. They were also in a new and unexpected situation, so an element of panic entered in.

Pendulum falls are often more risky than vertical falls of the same distance. The energy of the fall is similar but there is a higher chance of injuring head, trunk, or pelvis instead of an ankle. Protection skill, not climbing skill, was more important to Greg's accident—always protect a traverse for both the leader and the second. Joe was smart to move his anchor higher, but it wasn't enough. Greg may have been able to set solid pro in that crack partway across the traverse, leave the rope clipped through it until he was safely across, then pull the rope and leave the pro behind. Where possible, a less expensive option is to climb down well below Joe and then tension across. There are other simple solutions too numerous to describe here.

Regarding helmets, Joe said, "The thought of falling never entered our heads," yet both took serious falls on this moderate route. They also assumed that being the only party on the climb avoided the risk of rockfall, but Greg was below another climber (Joe) on every pitch and both were exposed to debris every time they pulled their rappel rope.

Ideally, Greg should have been immobilized right where he landed, in case of spinal injury. However, draped over a tree trunk 14 pitches up the climb with night falling is not an ideal setting. Would you know how to handle this situation? Wilderness First Responder training will help. [See also Bishops Terrace in this issue of ANAM.] Another serious risk from head trauma is intracranial bleeding, which may develop over several hours. The only treatment is fast transport to the neurosurgeon. Even if a rescue in the dark were not possible, and it often is, rescuers could at least have gotten basic medical care to Greg that night. They could have flown him off the route soon after dawn, shaving several hours off his time to the hospital.

But how to get help? Joe didn't realize his voice would be heard in the Valley, but it probably would have been. Making lots of noise is the best action in a situation like this. Second, he could have tried his FRS radio "in the blind" (to no one in particular). The NPS does not monitor these channels but many private users do. Third, he could have flashed an SOS if he had had a light. Fourth, something that in fact was done, is telling someone where he and Greg were going and when to begin to worry. In fact, the NPS was looking for them. (Source: Joe Hardy, Greg McFalls, John Dill, NPS Ranger, Yosemite National Park, and Jed Williamson.)

(Editor's Note: In September, two climbers—inexperienced—repeated this accident. They became stranded because they forgot to untie the safety knot in one end of the rappel rope, so it got stuck and they were stranded and benighted. They yelled for help. NPS personnel rescued them because it was a cold night.)

FALL ON ROCK—INADEQUATE BELAY, ROPE TOO SHORT—LOWERING, DISTRACTION
California, Yosemite Valley, Yin Yang

On April 26, an experienced climber (44) had led Yin Yang (5.10d) and set up a top-rope for his partner (26) to follow. The leader had used long cordelettes to extend the anchor because the climb was about 120 feet and their rope was only 200 feet. With the rope doubled, the leader was lowered safely to the ground because the anchor was extended. His partner top-roped the climb and disassembled the anchor. She threaded the rope through the anchor chain and her partner began to lower her. Her plan was to get to the end of the rope and swing over to another climb and down-climb a crack to the ground, a distance of about 15 feet. She was cleaning gear (stoppers) from the climb as she was being lowered. After she had done the retrievals from the crack, her partner began to lower her. As he did, the end of the rope fed through his belay device (an ATC), thereby resulting in a 20-foot fall to the ground. No serious injury resulted.

Analysis

The leader indicated that he did not have a knot tied in the end of the rope to prevent the rope from feeding through the belay device. He also said he was distracted by his partner's activity of extracting the stoppers, which were difficult to get out. (Source: David Horne, Yosemite Park Ranger)

(Editor's Note: Several lowering accidents have been reported each year over the last decade or so. Another one follows this one! Help get the word out to everyone that having a safety knot in the end of the rope is a given, but most importantly, be sure the rope is long enough for the job. Also note that if a knot IS tied in the end of the rope, the belayer still has to control the lowering. It's obvious that if the rope is not long enough, by 20 feet or more, then loss of control on the belay will STILL result in a fall that could lead to injury. Also, consider wearing gloves.

The person who was being lowered had some additional comments: I asked the third party to tie the knot when I was about 15-20 feet up, not from the top of the climb. Incidentally, the third party had previously been using the same set up, i.e. 60m. rope to TR the climb. This is an important detail to me because these were "experienced climbers" as well, all YOSAR folk and acquaintances. I think it created a bit of an "if everyone is doing it, it's OK" atmosphere. It was a good, if hard, lesson in trusting my instincts and taking responsibility for myself as well as the choices I make when it comes to climbing and safety.)

FALL ON ROCK—INADEQUATE BELAY (INCLUDING NO KNOT IN THE END OF THE CLIMBING ROPE), NO HARD HAT
California, Tahquitz Rock, Whodunit

On May 23, my partner and I had just arrived at the base of Whodunit (5.9) about 9:00 a.m. A female belayer (c. 25) was at the base of the route. She began to lower her partner (male, c. 25), who had just finished leading the first pitch of the route. It was not clear to us as to why the decision was made to lower rather than continue.

The belayer allowed the end of the rope to pass through her belay device, so her partner fell—a sliding, tumbling fall—about 40 feet and landed at her feet. He suffered a fractured arm, dislocated shoulder, and assorted abrasions/lacerations. Despite not wearing a helmet, there were no head or neck injuries.

Five of us (including his partner) were able to get him to the parking area, where he was able to be transported to medical treatment. (Source: Michael Morley)

FALL ON ROCK—RAPPEL ANCHOR FAILURE
California, High Sierra, Palisades Region

On May 29, Dan Kipper (54) and Warren Buettner (65) started from Glacier Camp and ascended the Palisade Glacier to the V-Notch. Their objective was to climb the V-notch, ascend Polemonium Peak, traverse over to Sill, and then descend back to camp. Snow and ice conditions, however, were not ideal. Fresh snow impeded the approach, and conditions on the V-Notch were crusty junk over blue ice. Dan did all the leading, as Warren was not at all comfortable on technical ice. Their progress was slow. They didn't top out until almost five o'clock.

Due to the late hour, they decided to forego Polemonium and Sill and head back down after taking a much-needed lunch break. They searched for the descent gully between Sill and the V-Notch, but couldn't locate it. They settled upon a gully that they knew was not the correct one, but one which looked like it would get them down to third-class rock after two or three rappels. (This gully is one gully north of the normal descent). They set up a sling anchor around two big horns; Dan went first and Warren followed. This got them to a ledge, where it looked like one or maybe two more rappels would get them onto third-class and then the glacier. However, when Dan tried to retrieve the rappel line, the rope jammed. They pulled on it for some time and finally gave up. Tying into the rope on a self-belay, Dan hauled himself back up a steep blocky face about forty feet high. There was a ledge here and he was able to free the ropes from this spot.

At this point, Dan said that he was setting up another anchor so that he could rappel back down to Warren. From there, he said, he was certain they could reach the third-class section with one more rappel. Warren waited several minutes in silence. Then Dan hollered, "Rope!" and threw down the ends. A minute or so later, Dan told him he was coming down. According to Warren, there was no sign of stress or concern in his voice. Then suddenly he heard him shout, "Oh no!" and Dan came plunging down, rope and all. It was a long fall—approximately 1,000 feet, to the bergshrund. Dan was killed instantly.

Night was setting in and with no rope or gear, Warren bivvied on the ledge. He yelled for help for some time but finally gave up. He could see Dan's body way down the glacier. He said it never moved. In the morning, he finally gathered enough courage to pick his way down the blocky face, convinced he was going to fall to his death at any moment, and eventually reached the glacier. He went down to Dan's body and stayed there with him for quite a while. Then he got up and hiked out to call the sheriff.

During the body recovery, it was noted that Dan's rappel device was properly attached to the rope and harness. A single sewn runner was looped through the top of the rope, suggesting that the sling had been cinched around a block or flake and had somehow popped free. Also, Dan's rappel device was a foot or so from the anchor point, suggesting that as soon as he leaned back and weighted the line, something immediately gave way. One possibility is that the block or flake that Dan had slung peeled off when he leaned back. Warren indicated that no rocks come crashing down on him when Dan fell.

On Monday May 31, 2004, volunteers of the Inyo County Sheriff's Search and Rescue team, assisted by C.H.P. helicopter H-82 from Apple Valley, recovered Kipper's body. He was flown off the glacier and released to the Inyo County Coroner's Office.

Analysis

Both climbers were tired at the end of a long day and ready to get down. Dan was known as a meticulous and safe climber. We'll never know exactly what happened, but it appears that when he slung the block, the sling slipped off when he weighted this anchor. Given his experience, it is hard to say how he might have made such a simple but fatal mistake. We can say that it is always a good policy to set a backup anchor while testing the primary rappel anchor prior to rappelling. (Source: Dave German, Inyo County SAR)

FALL ON ROCK, INADEQUATE PROTECTION, EXCEEDING ABILITIES
California, Tuolumne Meadows, Lembert Dome, Northwest Books

On July 15, Amit Singh (27) fell while climbing the third pitch (rated 5.9) of Northwest Books on Lembert Dome. He had placed a cam just above the belay and had started to climb the difficult section. Ten feet up, he placed a #5 nut and continued to climb another five to ten feet. He told me (park ranger) he had difficulty at the top of the crack, that he was struggling to hold on and place gear.

His partner, Anthony Baraff, said Singh struck his head and went unconscious for about 15 to 20 seconds. Singh could not remember what had happened. Baraff yelled for help and in about 15-20 minutes nearby climbers responded and went for help. Park rangers from the SAR team rescued Singh.

Analysis

These climbers had about two years of experience, mostly in the Gunks and mostly sport climbing. They were just starting trad climbing and said they were comfortable leading 5.7 to 5.8 routes.

The most important lesson here is that they were wearing helmets. (Source: George Paiva, Yosemite Valley SAR Ranger)

FALL ON ROCK—INADEQUATE PROTECTION (CLIMBER AND BELAYER), NO HARD HAT
California, Yosemite Valley, Church Bowl, Bishops Terrace

After work on July 28, Ric Sedlak (20) and I, Amy Painter (21), headed for the Church Bowl to climb Bishops Terrace (one pitch, 5.8). It was Ric's lead. He could follow 5.11, but he had just started leading traditional routes this summer and was learning protection skills on easier climbs. He'd led several other 5.8's so far with no problems. We bypassed the direct start and scrambled up to the large ledge where the right-hand variation begins about 50 feet above the ground. As he racked his gear I offered him a helmet—twice, but he just made a joke and shook his head at me. I reviewed some protection issues I thought important, and as he started up the crack he said I'd have to remind him to place enough pieces.

He placed a nut about ten feet directly above me and another a few feet higher. Then he continued straight up another ten feet or so to a small ledge. From there the climb goes left on foot holds for a few feet to the base of a large flake, then up a crack on either side of the flake to the crux higher on the pitch. Ric decided to wait until he reached the flake to place another piece. I suggested he at least put something at its base before starting up the cracks. Both sides of the flake would take protection. He started up the right side but decided the better of it, so he climbed down and traversed to the left side. I asked him again to put in a piece of protection. He must not have liked the left side of the flake any better than the right, because he decided to traverse back to the right and said, "Let me put in a piece on the right when I get back there." He still hadn't established protection beyond the first two nuts. At this point his waist was perhaps 15 feet above his highest piece and 15 feet left of it, and he was about 80 feet above the ground.

The two sides of the flake are six or seven feet apart, and the moves between the two, while not hard, require a bit of balance. Ric kept his left hand and foot on the left and stretched back to the right. It was far enough that he had to let go with his left hand, and when he realized that, he changed his mind. As he drew back to the left he must have somehow lost his balance, because he suddenly and involuntarily began to "barn door," swinging out as though his left hand and foot were the hinges of a door. He was looking directly to the right and down at me. We made eye contact and he said, "Oh shit! I'm going to fall!"

In the split second that I had I took in as much rope as possible, though nothing I could do would compensate for the deficiency in his protection. I saw his left hand come off. At the last second he thrust himself away from the wall to avoid scraping all the way down. He fell past me to the left and I heard him hit on the face below. I was not anchored and got yanked what seemed like five feet into the air. With rope stretch and all, he probably fell at least 30 to 40 feet.

I yelled Ric's name over and over, but got no reply. Holding him on belay, I moved left to the end of the ledge. Without re-rigging I started rappelling down the face using the belay device, with Ric as a counter-weight. Both of us were hanging from his protection at that point.

When I reached him he was unconscious, not responding to my calls, and hanging horizontally with his left side against the wall. I held myself in place with my right hand on my rappel line. I wedged myself between Ric and the wall and pushed him out with my left hand and my legs in order to look at his injuries.

That's when I saw all the blood running down the rock. A huge laceration ran from his right eyebrow up and across his forehead all the way to his left ear, and the flap of skin was folded forward, exposing his skull. I started yelling for help and almost immediately climbers answered from the west side of Church Bowl, "Keep yelling! We're coming! Where are you?" That gave me a bit of relief. All of this seemed to take only a minute from the time of Ric's fall.

By now my grip on the rope was slipping. I tried to wrap the rope around my leg, but I slipped lower until I was below Ric, so I gave up trying to help him and kept going 40 feet to the ground. I needed to get him down and stop the bleeding, so once I was on the ground I lowered him. As Ric came within reach, Tim, the first climber to arrive, cradled his body and laid him on his back.

By this time Ric had started to groan and respond to us. I tried to assess his mental status in more detail. I placed his scalp back in position, covered it with my folded tank top, and gently wrapped his head with Tim's shirt as a light pressure bandage. I knelt with his head between my knees to keep him still. Blood filled his mouth and nose (probably from skull fractures, I learned later) so he had to spit it out every couple of seconds to be able to breath. I was in the way, and I could still taste his blood hours later.

Someone had called 911. The medical clinic is only 400 yards away, so the ambulance crew arrived in couple of minutes, followed by the rescue team. Ric answered all their questions appropriately and he was soon bandaged, back-boarded, and aboard a medical helicopter headed to Modesto. In 30 minutes it would have been too dark to fly. At the hospital, x-rays and a CAT scan showed that his spine was OK, but his skull was fractured in three places—the frontal, left occipital, and right orbital bones. None required surgery, but it took 39 staples to close the big laceration plus lots of work on smaller cuts. He still does not remember the accident or the following several days, and he suffered neurological problems for a few weeks. They've since cleared up and he is climbing again.

Analysis

Ric should have followed Amy's advice by placing a piece as soon as he reached the right side of the flake. First, even though the moves were well within his abilities (and not even 5.8), mistakes do happen and he was facing a serious fall. Second, Amy had the belayer's perspective, which complements the leader's view. Third, she was the teacher. Better to overprotect when you're learning and then scale back as you gain skill than to learn the hard way. If nothing else, it gives the teacher something to critique.

Amy describes Ric as a natural athlete and seemingly fearless. Being on a relatively easy route may have given him too much confidence. This is pretty common among good athletes—until their first serious mishap.

It is indisputable that helmets prevent serious trauma from falls. Ric's was one of four serious accidents in Yosemite in 2004 affected by not wearing a helmet. [See McFalls (Royal Arches) and Singh (Lembert Dome) in this issue of ANAM.]

Amy pointed out later that she should have been anchored as she belayed. The belay ledge is big enough to walk around on safely, but she could have been injured and even dropped Ric as she was yanked upward into the wall. Furthermore, if Ric's pieces had failed, she could have been pulled off the ledge to the ground. Some climbers argue that anchoring the belayer increases the force on the protection, but that is dubious justification for risking the belayer, and one would not often apply that logic beyond the first pitch. If there is that much concern about the quality of the protection, the leader should place pieces closer together or assess whether or not to continue climbing.

Regardless of the situation, a first aid course like Wilderness First Responder, coupled with the self-rescue skills mentioned above, provide the tools to make informed, even though risky, decisions and to carry them out. (Source: Amy Painter and John Dill, NPS Ranger, Yosemite National Park)

FALL ON SNOW—INADEQUATE EQUIPMENT, OFF ROUTE, PARTY SEPARATED
California, High Sierra, Mount Ritter, Southeast Glacier

On August 9 the body of Otto Loenneker was found by Mono County Mountain Search and Rescue at the base of the Southeast Glacier on Mount Ritter.

Otto and his partner, John Dickinson, arrived at the base of Mount Ritter late morning of August 8. Their plan that day was to scout a route to the base of the Southeast Pinnacle, then return to basecamp. The "official" route ascends the 1,000 foot lower gully to the Southeast Pinnacle at the base of Ritter's Southeast Glacier, traverses north and back west around the edge of the glacier to Owen's Chute, then approaches the summit from the southwest. As they approached the gully, Otto and John disagreed about the location of the lower gully, with Otto starting up a line farther to the northwest. They agreed to rejoin at the base of the Southeast Pinnacle. When John arrived at the point where the route traverses, he looked down and saw Otto about 500 to 1,000 feet below him in the lower gully and assumed that his line had topped out on this other gully and that he had retreated to a point where he switched to the lower gully. John built a cairn to mark the turning point, then continued the traverse to a small snowfield below the Southeast Glacier. This was the last time he saw Otto alive.

Upon retracing his path, he did not encounter Otto and assumed that he had returned to basecamp. Not finding him there, he waited out the night in camp, then hiked out the next morning and requested SAR assistance. By 4:00 p.m. that afternoon, the Mono County Mountain SAR team, after several passes around Mounts Banner and Ritter in an Air National Guard Blackhawk, had a faint spotting on the lower portion of the Southeast Glacier. One team was put in lower down and climbed to the scene to find Otto's body in the rocks at the base of the glacier. A second team was inserted just before dark, to assist in packaging and lowering to a safe landing zone. All were retrieved the following morning.

Analysis

The most likely assessment of the events of that day is that Otto continued climbing up, missing the landmarks for the northwest traverse and instead headed up a steep gully to the east of the Southeast Pinnacle. This gully exits high on the glacier. It may have appeared to Otto that the glacier was partially snow-covered; however, it was in fact hard sastrugi. At this point, Otto, not seeing his partner John, may have believed that contrary to plan, he had gone for the summit that day. Regardless, despite lack of crampons and ice ax, he attempted to traverse high across the 35-degree glacier. At some point he lost his footing and slid approximately 500 feet into the rocks.

Teams should be extremely cautious about splitting up, especially when on unfamiliar terrain. The conditions high on the Southeast Glacier, which Otto attempted to traverse, were hard ice laced with encrusted rock shards. Faced with such conditions, without proper equipment and contrary to agreed upon plans, Otto should have retreated. (Source: Craig Knoche, Mono County Mountain SAR)

FALL ON ROCK, WEATHER, INADEQUATE PROTECTION—RAPPEL ANCHOR CAME OFF, INADEQUATE EQUIPMENT
California, High Sierra, Middle Palisade

At 4:15 a.m. on August 14, experienced climbers Alfred Fordiani (43) and Dave Brummund (42) left their Brainard Lake camp with a choice of climbs depending on the weather, which had been unsettled for the past several days. If excellent weather, they would attempt the Eagle Face of Norman Clyde Peak (5.4, approximately 1,000 feet of technical climbing, descent by 3rd/4th class NF/NNE ridge); or in the event of iffy weather, they would attempt the East Face of Middle Palisade (3rd class).

At 8:00 a.m. the weather looked excellent, and the pair traversed the knife-edged lowest section of Norman Clyde's NNE ridge onto the Eagle Face, avoiding the first cliff band directly above the Middle Pal Glacier. They started up the face climbing with rock shoes and a single 60-meter rope, leaving boots, ice ax, and crampons by the big snowfield on the face of Norman Clyde.

By 1:00 p.m., the climbers were about 1.5 rope lengths from the top of the face, but dark clouds were building. They hurried to make it off of the face before the weather came in, but rain and hail started falling as they began the last short (½ rope length) pitch. Fordiani was leading about 15 feet from the top of the face and attempted to mantle over a large block. But the block was covered with hail and offered no purchase. Attempting instead to climb a slightly more difficult flake to the left, the flake broke off, and he took a leader fall of approximately 30 feet, wrenching his left knee and severely bruising his pelvis and left quadriceps. Brummond lowered him back to the belay stance, and it was agreed that given the conditions of both the face and Fordiani, there was no way to continue climbing to the top. They rappelled back down the face, using a combination of old anchors and new. The descent, while slow with a single rope, went without incident down to the snowfield where they gathered up their boots and snow gear.

Fordiani was mobile at this point, but slow and a bit unsteady due to his left leg injuries. The rain and hail had ended but the rock was still wet. It was decided to bypass the knife-edge on descent and instead rappel the last cliff band to the talus/glacier on the Middle Palisade—three single rope rappels. The first two rappels went without incident, and a 5' by 5' triangular block was slung for the final rappel to the talus. Brummund rapped down, and Frodiani followed. Darkness was just arriving. Fordiani reached the talus and was walking backwards down the talus still on rappel tension when the rappel block broke free from the cliff, initiating a significant rockfall. Fordiani tumbled backwards and attempted to roll out of the way, but the rappel block landed on his leg, breaking his right ankle.

It was clear that it was a rescue situation. Brummund made sure his partner was stable and comfortable with food, water, and warm clothes, and headed back to Brainard Lake camp, arriving at 11:30 p.m. After a few hours sleep, he headed down the trail, arriving at Glacier Lodge 10:00 a.m. Sunday morning. The sheriff was phoned, initiating rescue. Fordiani was rescued by Inyo County SAR by helicopter at 2:00 p.m. He had surgery on his ankle and should make a full recovery.

Analysis

Alfred Fordiani wrote a lengthy analysis which is summarized below.

I was convinced that the moisture had blown out, and that all-day sun was in store for us. This was clearly an error, and I should have realized that the clouds in the valley were an indication of moisture that might rain on us... It is worth noting that we were probably off-route at the top of the face. The route description (Roper, Secor) seemed to make it clear that there was some careful route finding to be done at the top of the route; in our haste to get to the top we did not take the time to look around, but rather took the first line that seemed climbable... In hindsight, I wish that we had scouted a bit to be sure that we were on the easiest route.

The move on which I fell was well protected with a bomber #2 Camalot. I was only six or seven feet above my piece when I fell, and so should have fallen at most, 15-18 feet. In 18 years of climbing with D.B., I have tried to climb well within my abilities and have never taken a leader fall (outside of sport climbing), so D.B. was caught a bit by surprise by my fall and let a half a second or so of rope through the belay before checking my fall. While I knew that I was making a somewhat awkward move out of his line of sight, I did not warn D.B. to watch me. I was surprised when my hold broke, but it was a tricky enough situation that I certainly should have warned him to watch me.

I have found that as I have gotten older, I have progressively tried to go lighter and lighter, and being fresh at the end of the day is safety. But this I will say: given the stress of finding suitable rap anchors, I will never again venture onto an alpine face, even an easy one, without a few pitons and a hammer for use in emergency. As it goes, all of the factors leading to and including the leader fall and tedious rappel descent of the face are to me just part of climbing and in my opinion well within the realm of acceptable risk. I misread the weather a bit and paid a small price. If the leader fall and rap down the face was all there was to the story, I would have walked out, albeit slowly with my pelvis and left leg injuries, defeated on the climb and banged up a bit, but without a story to tell.

The rap anchor failure at the very bottom is something else entirely. We probably would have rapped that little cliff even if we had finished the face and descended the standard route without incident. Many years of reading Accidents in North America (sic) have taught me that rap anchor failure equals death, and I should be dead. I am beyond shocked that the anchor failed. We pushed on that block with our whole might and it didn't budge. I watched D.B. rap down on that block and it didn't budge a micrometer. Why it came down when it did I don't know, but it scares me to think about it. Last year I climbed a couple of peaks in Canada that have maintained rap stations with big, fat double bolts and rings. I like those.

One final note: The space blanket that I have carried for many years finally came into use and worked very well. I strongly recommend that every climber carry one. (Source: From a report submitted by Dave German)

FALL ON ROCK, PLACED NO PROTECTION
California, High Sierra, Middle Palisade

On August 22, a group of eight Sierra Club members were ascending the Northeast Face of Middle Palisade (3rd class). The party was moving adequately, but slowly. The party was unroped. All members of the party were wearing helmets. Near the top of the first chute, where the route bears left, they met with two other parties descending the route. The descending parties, one guide with two clients (roped) and one solo climber, set about passing the group. At some time during this transition, Brian Reynolds (31), who was facing the cliff, stepped back one step too far and fell backwards. Brian landed headfirst 30 feet down and continued to fall until he was out of sight. All three groups descended to check on Brian's condition, while calling the Inyo County Sheriff's office for Search and Rescue support. There was a trail of blood leading downwards. At the base of the route, just above the Norman Clyde Glacier, Brian was found. He was pronounced dead immediately. Inyo SAR arrived within about one hour and verified Brian's condition as deceased.

Additional SAR team members were inserted to assist, while the climbing parties continued their descent to Brainard Lake. Due to high winds and deteriorating weather conditions, the body recovery was postponed until the following day. Early the following day, the body was flown out via long line.

Analysis

The route is steep and dangerous. It is nominally rated as 3rd class, but a fall is likely to be fatal due to the steep nature of the terrain. Passing of other climbers can be hazardous because of the positioning. Being able to anchor in when passing other climbers is always a consideration. (Source: Dave German)

FALL ON ROCK–JUMPED INSTEAD OF DOWN-CLIMBING
California, Yosemite National Park, Tuolumne Meadows, Matthes Crest

On August 25, Mark Sorenson (38) and David Parrish (38) were climbing Matthes Crest and were about at the halfway point when this accident happened. Parrish had led an easy pitch for about 50 feet, placing no protection along the way, as it was easy 3rd class. Parrish recalls yelling, "Off belay," to Sorenson, who waved to him indicating he understood. Parrish then put Sorenson on belay using an ATC. He could see Sorenson coming his way, but then he went out of sight. Parrish was taking in rope as fast as he could, but never felt the rope come taut. Then he heard Sorenson yell something, then felt the rope come tight on him. He looked over his left shoulder and saw Sorenson lying on a ledge with his foot bleeding. Parrish tied him off and climbed down to him. He could see that the foot was broken and severely deformed.

Another climbing party rappelled and ran six miles to report the accident. SAR personnel called in a helicopter. Sorenson was shorthauled off, then put in the helicopter and flown to mammoth Lakes Hospital. (Source: From a report by George Paiva, SAR Ranger)

Analysis

Both climbers were experienced. Sorenson was out-climbing his belayer's ability to keep the rope taut on the relatively easy terrain. Sorenson had gone off the 3rd class terrain and on to a 5.7 section. He chose to jump out and then onto a sloped ledge four feet down, rather than down-climbing.

John Dill conducted an interview with both climbers. From that ten page document, the following from Mark Sorenson sums it all up:

"I would say that my mistake was being impatient, and feeling it was an easy climb. Perhaps I didn't take it serious enough, because everything is serious. If you've been climbing for a long time and you're on something well below your top level... I don't want to say we were lackadaisical, we were even wearing helmets up there, although there's no chance of a rock hitting you in the head because there's no one above you.

"We discussed *Touching the Void*... if you're that far out and you break a leg...

"I actually considered how I might rap with my foot like that. I could probably one-foot it down, find a stick for a crutch, but David was telling me, 'No, you're not going anywhere. Don't worry about it, we'll get the helicopter up here.' Once the shadows started getting long I started thinking I might be out there all night. If they didn't get to me when they did, I probably would have lost the foot.

"One lesson is: no matter how easy the climb is you have to pretend it's the hardest thing you ever did."

STRANDED—BENIGHTED (LATE START), INADEQUATE CLOTHING AND EQUIPMENT, EXCEEDING ABILITIES
California, Yosemite National Park, Tuolumne Meadows, Lembert Dome
On September 7 at 2030, Philip Kast (22) and Sean McCarthy (25) were benighted and ledged out on Lembert Dome after a technical rock climb on the northwest face. They topped out just at nightfall and began traversing east along easy 4th class terrain. They had only one headlamp and were dressed in shorts and t-shirts. About 2245, they found themselves on the Southwest Face in 5th class terrain and unable to navigate the descent. They attempted to lead climb up to the top but found no protection placements available. They decided to stay where they were and call for help. A nearby hiker in the parking lot heard their cries for help and saw their flashing headlamp.

Rangers conducted a technical rescue response, doing a 300-foot lower. (Source: From a report by George Paiva, SAR Ranger)

(Editor's Note: A few of these happen every year in various locations. One or two are always included as reminders of some obvious factors. See September 19 and 26 below also.)

FALL ON ROCK, FAILURE TO BACKUP ASCENDERS
California, Yosemite Valley, El Capitan, Tangerine Trip
On September 8, Jeff Cabral (33) fell to his death while following the fifth pitch of Tangerine Trip (Grade VI, 5.8 A2/C3) on the Southeast Face of El

Capitan. At least four other people have died while cleaning aid pitches on El Cap, and Jeff's death echoed that of Carol Moyer on this same route in 1983. We will never know exactly what caused Jeff's fatal fall, but like most other jugging accidents we know that it could have been easily prevented.

On Tuesday the 7th, Jeff and his two partners, Chris Lamme (30) and Nick Tyler (30), fixed the first four pitches of the route and spent the night on the ground. Early Wednesday morning the team jugged to their high point, planning to finish the route in four or five days. While Jeff and Nick hauled their bags up from the base of the wall, Chris began rope-soloing the fifth pitch. This pitch follows a steep crack system up and left above a roof, traverses about fifty feet over its 160-foot length, and overhangs slightly from start to finish. After Chris finished leading, Nick lowered out from the belay and jugged up a free hanging tag line to join him. Jeff then released the haul bag from the belay and began cleaning the pitch while the pair above hauled.

According to Chris and Nick, Jeff was quite frustrated while cleaning the pitch, but given its steep angle, this wasn't much of a surprise. Anyone who has cleaned a traversing aid pitch knows the process can be tedious and exasperating. Despite his frustration, Jeff moved up the pitch steadily without asking for help or advice from his partners above. When he was about thirty feet from the top anchor, both Chris and Nick heard what sounded like a piece "popping" (unexpectedly pulling out of the crack). Chris was looking down at Jeff at the time (though he couldn't see Jeff's gear or ascenders) and saw him swing awkwardly left before starting to fall. Chris watched Jeff "slide" down the rope and "pause," or jerk, near its end before falling free of the rope and continuing to the ground five hundred feet below.

The majority of their rack fell with Jeff, and after witnessing his fall, Chris and Nick were not confident they could safely retreat down the overhanging route. They spent that night on the wall and were assisted to the ground by Yosemite's rescue team the following morning.

Analysis

Somehow both of Jeff's ascenders came off the rope. He was either not backed up to that rope or his backup method failed. He was using a relatively new set of Petzl ascenders with adjustable daisies and each of his ascenders appeared to be in working order after the accident. When they were found, Jeff's right ascender was locked open and the left one was closed; that is, the cam was engaged as it would be when fixed on a rope. One locking carabiner (locked) was attached to his belay loop, and a Grigri self-belay device was clipped to the strap connecting his two leg loops. Like his ascenders, this Grigri was in fine working order after Jeff's fall, and based on a variety of factors it was likely never attached to the line Jeff was ascending.

After the accident, the rope Jeff had been ascending ran from the top anchor down through a number of pieces before hanging free in space. A figure eight on a bight was tied about 25 feet from its lower end as one might tie to "clip in short" while cleaning an aid pitch. This knot was deformed, having clearly taken a strong impact, but it was not deformed as one would expect had it been pulled from the "bight" side. Rather, it appeared Jeff had slid down the rope and hit the knot, thereby tightening it (as well as tightening the clove hitch anchoring that rope above) without pulling on the actual bight.

Before attempting Tangerine Trip, Jeff climbed the Prow on Washington Column, routes in Zion, and various other moderate aid lines (though it's unclear how experienced he was at cleaning traverses). According to his partners, Jeff knew to tie into the lead-line when cleaning an aid pitch. The carabiner on his belay loop along with the figure-eight knot in the rope suggest that he at least intended to back himself up. Something did keep Jeff "attached" to the lead line as he slid down its length (possibly a snarled daisy chain or a carabiner clipped in an unusual arrangement), but whatever this attachment, it was not enough to stop his fall.

Many different scenarios could have caused Jeff's fall, and exactly how his ascenders came off the line will remain a mystery. Cleaning a traversing aid pitch is an awkward process and it's easy to accidentally cross weight or tweak ascenders in the balancing act. The slight shock caused by a piece popping might have loaded his system in an unusual way, or Jeff may have intentionally removed one or even both ascenders to lower out or otherwise pass an awkward placement. Regardless, the lesson remains the same: If Jeff had tied or clipped in effectively to the lead line below his ascenders, he would have been caught.

All climbers bend rules occasionally, but backing yourself up while cleaning a traverse is one rule that should hold fast. Tying into the end of the lead line is a good habit (one that might have saved Jeff's life on this overhanging route), but this "if all else fails" backup leaves room for disaster in a long fall. In 1980 Walter Bertsch fell a full rope-length while jugging on Magic Mushroom and died, despite being caught by his lead-line. The essential precaution is to tie in short as you move up the pitch, especially if the pitch is traversing or awkward. Tie a figure-eight knot on a bight just below you on the lead-line and clip it to a locking carabiner on your harness (as Jeff may have intended). As you ascend, periodically tie a new knot in the rope and clip it to another locker before unclipping the previous one. The more frequently you clip in, the shorter your potential fall.

It's also possible to back up ascenders with a self-belay device (as Jeff might have intended to do with his Grigri). When used correctly, these tools can provide a convenient and effective backup. Be careful though, as some devices can damage or even cut a climbing rope under the force of a fall. The bottom line: Don't trust your life to ascenders alone. Before leaving the ground, decide on a backup method, practice it, and stick to it once you're on the wall. With a little experience, it won't slow you down, and it might save your life. (Source: Lincoln Else, Yosemite Climbing Ranger)

WEATHER, STRANDED—BENIGHTED, INADEQUATE CLOTHING AND EQUIPMENT, EXHAUSTION
California, Yosemite National Park, Tuolumne Meadows, Fairview Dome

On September 19, two Japanese climbers, Kengo Tagai (31) and Akira Uasa (39), began ascending Fairview Dome at 0830. when they reached the 4th class area of the route (about 2-300 feet from the top), they were exhausted and the rock was wet from snow-fall. They were unable to complete the route, and as they only had one rope, were unable to descend. They spent the night huddled under a nylon tarp on a ledge. They had no bivouac gear.

On the following day, Tagai climbed out, but Uasa was unable to follow. Akira Uasa was short hauled off, then helicoptered to Mammoth Hospital for treatment for kidney failure. Kengo Tagai had frostbitten toes and swollen feet, but suffered no permanent damage. (Source: From an NPS SAR report)

STRANDED—INEXPERIENCE
California, Yosemite National Park, Tuolumne Meadows, Tenaya Peak

On September 26, Marvin and Mary Kilgo (both 42) became stranded about three or four pitches from the top of Tenaya Peak. They requested help. Another climbing party reported this to rangers, who responded by rappelling down to them.

The Kilgos had adequate clothing and equipment, but had limited outdoor climbing experience. The rangers set up a top-rope situation for them, so they were able to climb to the top.

(Editor's Note: Two more examples of being stranded—for different reasons, but with the common denominator of being in a new and unexpected situation.)

STRANDED BY WEATHER—INADEQUATE GEAR, FOOD, AND STRATEGY
California, Yosemite Valley, El Capitan

Just before midnight on October 16, a cold front brought heavy rain to Yosemite Valley. Several climbing parties managed to retreat from big wall routes, but four teams caught high on the face of El Capitan were stranded by what became a four-day winter storm. Three of these parties survived long enough to be rescued by the National Park Service, but two climbers died from hypothermia three pitches from the top of the Nose. This account summarizes the problems the parties faced and the roles that preparation, strategy, and luck played in the outcome. First of all, here is a description of the situation on each route:

Tempest. On Monday, October 4, two weeks before the storm began,

Dave Turner (22) started up Tempest (Grade VI, 5.10 A4). This was his sixteenth climb and tenth solo of El Cap. He had climbed it twice in winter, had soloed it in a day, and had experienced severe weather on at least one previous El Cap climb. When the storm arrived on his 13th day on Tempest, Turner was three pitches from the summit.

Never Never Land. A week later, on Monday the 11th, Tommy Thompson (40) and Erik Erickson (49) started up Octopussy (Grade VI, 5.9 A3+), a route that joins Never Never Land before topping out on Lurking Fear. Thompson and Erickson had almost 70 El Cap ascents between them, including some of Yosemite's hardest aid lines. Both are experienced mountaineers, and both have endured previous storms on El Cap. After hearing of a chance of rain later in the week, they cancelled plans for a longer route and chose the shorter alternative. They intended to finish in five days, but the route proved harder than expected and when the storm hit on their sixth night they were still three pitches short of the top.

The Salathé Wall. On Wednesday the 13th, four days before the storm, Tom Andrews (44) and Marisol Monterrubio Velasco (22), started up the Salathé Wall (Grade VI, 5.9 C2). Andrews, an AMGA guide with extensive mountaineering experience, had climbed several walls including the Nose on El Cap. Velasco, from Santo Torras, Mexico, had climbed long routes in Peru as well as the Nose and Half Dome. They figured the Salathé would take them five days. They stayed on schedule, but on their fourth night the storm pinned them down on Sous le Toit ledge with seven pitches to go.

The Nose. On Thursday the 14th, Ryoichi Yamamoto (26) and Mariko Ryugo (27), both from Hyogo, Japan, started up the Nose (Grade VI, 5.9 C2). Yamamoto was a talented free climber and Ryugo was a competent follower, though inexperienced compared to Yamamoto. Their only aid climbing experience was a recent ascent of Washington Column, where Ryugo apparently led her first pitch. They probably planned to spend four or five days on the Nose. Yamamoto led every pitch and they made good time, keeping pace with a party above them. By the end of their third day they were bivouacked at Camp 6, five pitches below the summit, with all or part of the next pitch fixed. The party ahead of them pressed on after dark and reached the top just as the first wave of rain arrived.

The Rescues. It rained four inches on Sunday the 17th and low clouds covered El Cap for most of the day. On the afternoon the 18th the clouds lifted for a few hours, allowing rangers on the Valley floor a view of the face. Everywhere on the wall, streams of water ran off the summit and blew sideways in the wind. Although conditions were clearly miserable, none of the four parties the rangers could see appeared to be asking for a rescue and no one in the Valley reported friends in need of help. Monday night the rain returned.

By the morning the 19th, snow coated the Valley rim. Thompson and Erickson on Never Never Land and Turner on Tempest relayed through friends by FRS (family band) radio that they were OK for the moment, but Turner was losing confidence as he continued to get colder. Nothing was known about the Salathé and Nose parties at this point, including names, experience, and gear, but the Salathé team appeared to be sheltered in a portaledge.

Visibility remained poor all morning. Efforts continued to get information about the Nose team, and late Tuesday morning rangers finally tracked down a Japanese climber who knew them. With this climber translating through a loud speaker, the NPS tried to communicate with them. One possible responding call was heard but nothing more. Nevertheless, given the weather and what rangers now knew about this team, it was clear that if a rescue were not needed already it would be soon. Preparations began immediately for a large operation supported by additional rescuers from outside the park. Given the weather, helicopter assistance was out of the question. By 3 p.m. an advanced ground party was hiking and snow shoeing through deep powder toward the summit, a distance of about 11 miles. About the same time, a break in the clouds allowed spotters with a telescope to see a climber (probably Yamamoto) about two pitches above Camp 6, apparently trying to wrap himself in a yellow tarp. Two hours later another break showed what looked like two people, motionless, with the tarp partially unwrapped and blowing in the wind.

Despite attempts to hike through the night, harsh conditions and low visibility kept rescue teams from reaching the summit until late morning on Wednesday the 20th. As they arrived, Turner on Tempest radioed that he had become significantly hypothermic and might not survive another night on the wall. By this time visibility had improved. It was obvious to NPS observers in the Valley that the Nose party was deceased, so the summit team turned its attention to Turner. When a rescuer was lowered to him, Turner was able to jumar up the NPS ropes unassisted.

In mid-afternoon, not long after Turner had reached safety, Thompson and Erickson on Never Never Land also radioed for help. They assured the NPS that they could stay on the wall until the next day, so rescuers fixed lines down the slabs to the rim above them and returned to their basecamp on the summit for the night.

[From the summit of El Capitan, several hundred feet of granite slabs slope down to the rim, where the vertical face begins. In the storm's early stages the slabs ran with water and as temperatures dropped they became coated with ice and snow. Rescuers were forced to begin fixing lines much farther from the edge than they normally would if the rock were dry.]

On Thursday morning the 21st the rescuers split into two teams. One team descended their fixed lines and lowered two rescuers to the Never

Never Land party. Thompson and Erickson were able to ascend the lines under their own power and reached the summit by mid-afternoon. Meanwhile, the second team lowered a rescuer to the Nose party. After he had investigated the scene, the bodies of Yamamoto and Ryugo were raised to the summit. In early afternoon, while these operations were continuing, Andrews and Velasco began signaling for a rescue from the Salathé. By the time personnel and equipment could be released from the Nose and Never Never Land and moved into position, it was clear that the Salathé operation would take the rescue team well into the night. Because of ice on the slabs and runoff on the face, the team decided to delay the rescue until the next day. The park helicopter was able to deliver a haul-bag of food and dry clothes directly to the Salathé party just before dark, ensuring that they could spend a more comfortable night on the wall. On the 22nd, six days after the storm had begun, a rescuer was lowered to Andrews and Velasco and they were raised to the summit in good condition.

What follows next are the stories from each party.

Tempest. Dave Turner was equipped with a Black Diamond two-person portaledge and an A5 rain fly (both borrowed), a Bibler big wall bivy sack, a synthetic sleeping bag (rated to 25 degree F) with a fleece liner, two sleeping pads, Gore-Tex raingear, warm synthetic layers, a butane stove, and an FRS radio. He had no winter hat or waterproof gloves.

The ledge and fly were in excellent condition but of different brands and the fly did not provide sufficient overlap. By the time he awoke Sunday morning Turner was in a puddle. "[My friend] said they would probably be compatible," he said, "but I did not check this on the ground—I should have." He managed to slow the leaks with garbage bags but then he discovered water dripping through the unsealed seam of the pole sleeve that ran the length of the fly.

Turner had several days of food and water left, so he initially felt comfortable waiting out the weather. "I was only slightly damp and only three pitches from the summit, " he said. "I figured it would clear up in a day or two." Nevertheless, he was already wet, in a leaky shelter, and facing three more storm days on the way.

When the rain let up briefly on Monday afternoon, Turner made a dash for the top. Water poured down the dihedral he was climbing. His progress was slow and each time he raised an arm to place gear, water ran into the cuff of his jacket. In his hurry to get moving he had left his rope bag cinched too tight, forcing him to retreat from half way up the pitch to release a snagged rope. "A rookie mistake," he said later. By nightfall he had managed to fix one pitch above his ledge, but the effort had left him soaked and mildly hypothermic. Attempts to dry his clothes and keep warm with his butane stove proved fruitless. When it snowed heavily Monday night, he realized that the two slab pitches above would now be impassible and that runoff from snowmelt would continue after the storm cleared. On Tuesday night the temperature dropped further and he shivered continuously. By Wednesday morning he was losing sensation and function in his hands and feet. He knew he could not spend another night on the wall so he radioed for help.

Never-Never Land. Thompson and Erickson left the ground with solid storm gear: an A5 Cliff Cabana two-person portaledge with expedition rain fly, Gore-Tex bivy sacks, 0 degree F synthetic sleeping bags, sleeping pads, full Gore-Tex rain gear, and warm synthetic layers. Like Turner, they were not too worried at the start of the storm. However, their situation deteriorated over the next four days as wind-driven rain worked through the ventilation port on their fly, condensation built up inside, and the drain holes in the floor proved inadequate. "I felt like we were in a row boat in the middle of a north Atlantic hurricane," Thompson said. "We had the best ledge money could buy, with a four-season fly that encompassed the whole thing. This system saved our lives, but even with everything set up right, we didn't have a single dry item to our name…and we slept in a puddle."

Unlike Turner, they did not try to leave their ledge to climb, and although they were cold, hypothermia never reached a critical point. However, they had packed only one day's extra rations and in the end they ran out of food and water. "We were already using our reserves before the storm hit," Thompson said. "We initially declined any rescue efforts, but with no food and no assurance we could climb the slabs above the lip even if the weather broke, Erik and I had to discuss the unspeakable—getting help." When they were finally rescued on Thursday, they hadn't eaten in three days.

Salathé. When Andrews and Velasco began their climb, the forecast called for clear skies with the possibility of cloudy weather in several days. They planned to bivy on natural ledges, but as a hedge they brought a one-person portaledge (an old, beat up, Gramicci prototype) with a new one-person Black Diamond rain fly. They also brought lots of warm synthetic layers, hats, gloves, and a butane stove. Andrews had full Gore-Tex rain gear and a sleeping bag but Velasco had neither—against his better judgment, Andrews had allowed her to leave her bag behind when she suggested that her bivy sack and extra fleece would be sufficient. Their supply of food and water was barely enough for the climb, so by the time they reached Sous le Toit ledge on Saturday, a little more than a day's worth remained.

When the rain started that night, they crammed themselves into the portaledge. Like everyone else on the wall they were soon wet from condensation and fighting to maintain their shelter against the wind. As temperatures dropped, chunks of snow and ice falling from the summit slammed into the fly. One strike broke the fly pole but Andrews managed to grab it before the jagged ends shredded the fabric. He and Velasco shared their one sleeping bag and bivy sack. As it got colder and their food ran out, they lived on lemon drops dissolved in hot water. Somehow their portaledge developed no major leaks, and in a stroke of luck, Sous le Toit ledge saw little runoff compared to the other parties. As a result, Andrews managed to fix two pitches during breaks in the weather.

By the time the storm ended mid-day Wednesday, they were cold and tired, but they initially turned down a rescue. "After much consideration and despite the urge to give up, we said no, that we were fine and would try to continue climbing," Andrews said. "Besides, I figured there had to be other teams in worse shape." At that point they still hoped to climb out the next day, but Thursday morning they awoke to find their fixed ropes, the portaledge, and the pitches above encased in a layer of ice. When the ice finally melted in the afternoon, they tried to lead the first headwall pitch but quickly recognized that they were exhausted, moving too slowly, and becoming dangerously sloppy with their rigging. Like Thompson and Erickson, lack of food was the primary factor that finally forced them to call for help, but the cold and the constant physical and psychological effort to keep their shelter together and their spirits up were close behind.

The Nose. Like the Salathé party, Yamamoto and Ryugo planned to sleep on natural ledges. They brought Gore-Tex bivy sacks, light-weight synthetic sleeping bags, sleeping pads, and a very light rain fly from a tent, but no portaledge. For warmth they had some synthetic layers but less than the other parties on the wall (for example, Ryugo had only thin nylon pants with no insulation). They also lacked waterproof rain shells and warm gloves.

They probably met the initial rain with dismay but not desperation. In dated photographs found in their digital camera they appear relatively comfortable at Camp 6 on Sunday morning. Like many Nose parties before them, however, they probably found that in storms, Camp 6 becomes the base of a funnel draining the dihedral above, and also that a tent fly is inadequate protection.

In the next (and last) set of photographs, taken Tuesday morning, Yamamoto is seen ascending their fixed line from Camp 6, apparently attempting to reach the summit. Based on evidence found at the scene, here is an educated guess at the subsequent events: Yamamoto stopped at the top of pitch 27 and Ryugo joined him. She belayed him as he led pitch 28, in conditions as bad or worse than Turner had experienced on Tempest the day before. Yamamoto completed pitch 28 and fixed his line. Then he descended, perhaps to help Ryugo after her long, cold belay at the anchor below.

They were now fully exposed to the storm. Their hands barely functioned and hypothermia was eroding their abilities both physically and mentally. In the hours that followed they appear to have changed strategies a number of times. Their lead line was now unavailable, rigged to the anchors above. In a final effort—either to descend to Camp 6 or to keep climbing—they cut their lead and haul lines in various places, possibly because their hands were too cold to untie the knots. Somehow, in the midst of their confusion, they dropped their haul line and haul bag with most of its contents, including insulation and food. They still had one sleeping bag and the tent fly, which Ryugo had been using for shelter while belaying, but the remainder of their bivy gear was now gone. They were found huddled together, wrapped in the fly, at an impromptu—but still logically arranged—belay, half way up pitch 28. They probably died Tuesday evening.

Analysis

Weather changes everything. Climbers don't leave their ropes and racks behind, but without threatening clouds overhead, most parties shortcut on storm gear in one way or another. The only reason to check the forecast in storm season is to decide whether it's worth starting the climb, not whether to bring full survival gear. Always distrust a sunny forecast and go fully equipped. Take along the means to receive updated forecasts—a weather radio, cell phone, or FRS radio. (See Communications, below.)

Shelter. A tent fly inherently leaks and can't be pitched properly. A portaledge fly alone is not much better, as previous El Cap climbers have discovered. A portaledge is essential. It must be in top condition, with all seams sealed and with a correctly fitting fly. One small leak over a couple of days can be disastrous. A portaledge would probably have kept Yamamoto and Ryugo alive.

Clothing. Because of condensation, even the best shelter will be wet eventually. Bivy sack, sleeping bag, warm clothes (including winter hats, gloves, and socks), and rain gear all extend survival time in a soggy portaledge or on rappel. Extra pairs of warm, waterproof gloves are crucial to the party's ability to function. Nothing dries out in 100 percent humidity, so all insulation must be rated for colder temperatures than may be encountered. Most parties also rely on hot drinks as another source of warmth. Finally, an under-equipped partner is a weak link for the whole team, so double-check each other's gear and don't allow shortcuts.

Food and water. The Salathé and Never Never Land parties were stopped primarily by lack of food. One day's cushion is not enough. First, overestimating one's climbing speed even in good weather is common. Second, severe multi-day storms in October are not unusual. Third, even if the storm is brief, impassable wet/icy slabs and run-off from melting snow can add a day or more to one's immobility. "We needed more than twice as much food and water than we had originally planned for," Tommy Thompson said. "Where do you draw the line?" The answer is: Unless you want others to bail you out, you have to be as thorough with calories as with the rest of your preparations. This isn't about gourmet dining. A tiny package of ten energy bars will cover one person's basic requirements for a day.

Strategy. Hindsight suggests that the best strategy for all parties, even for the Japanese climbers, would have been to stay in their shelters, out of the wind, and ride out the storm as best they could. Tom Andrews on the Salathé was able to climb safely during breaks in the storm only because his pitches happened to be fairly dry. Turner and the Japanese faced much worse conditions when they tried to climb and their clothing proved inadequate for the task. They needed sealed sleeves (e.g., kayak dry-top jackets), waterproof gloves that fit over the sleeves, and ample insulation. In addition, all four parties faced potentially ice-covered pitches during and <u>after</u> the storm, for which small pitons, hooks, and even bolts, might be required. (In 1984 two Japanese climbers died of hypothermia on the last pitch of the Nose, probably for lack of similar hardware. They had made a dash for the top in a storm without adequate clothing and shelter.)

However, the summit is only half-way to safety. Had Turner or the Japanese team reached the top, they would have found themselves in worse physical condition and facing deep snow, high wind, low visibility, and dangerous terrain. Negotiating the East Ledges descent from the summit of El Cap in these conditions is a life-threatening endeavor in itself.

Rappelling is another option, but like climbing out, it can not be taken for granted. According to their friends, Yamamoto and Ryugo chose the Nose partly because they could descend from any pitch on the route. When the time came to decide, however, they were already wet and they may have realized how exposed they would be to the weather and how dependent on finding every anchor.

Communications. Cell phones and radios degrade the wilderness character of a climb, but in a desperate situation those values may not seem so important. "I had never brought a radio or cell phone on El Cap before, and I will never *not* bring them again," said Thompson of Never Never Land. However, these devices are only an extension of the basic rule: Tell someone where you're going and when you'll be back. Even lacking a radio, an emergency plan with friends might have made the difference for Yamamoto and Ryugo. If all else fails, remember that cries for help—but not the details of a message—can be heard from the Valley floor. (Note: Some cell phones do not work in the park, and the NPS does not routinely monitor FRS radios.)

Don't count on a rescue. All the communication in the world won't guarantee a rescue in the time one has left to survive. "The question I keep asking myself," Thompson said, "is, what would we have done if there was no rescue team, if we were on some remote wall elsewhere?" To answer the question, imagine yourself on a wall only as "remote" as Half Dome, hidden by clouds, while the rescue team is focused on El Cap. A safe return depends on self-sufficiency. (Sources: Lincoln Else and John Dill, NPS Rangers, Yosemite National Park)

FALL ON ICE—ICE FOOTHOLD CAME OFF, ICE TOOLS CAME OUT, WEATHER
Colorado, Rocky Mountain National Park, Hidden Falls

On January 10, Steven Crane (57) was leading Main Falls Center I WI 4 (one pitch, 80 feet) when he fell about 30 feet. He had placed three ice screws prior to the fall. As he moved further on the upper column, he was sprayed by water coming off the right side of the falls. According to local sources, it had been a wetter than normal year at Hidden Falls.

Crane was wearing prescription glasses,which became all wet and fogged. He said that he eventually had no vision at all and began climbing by feel. The belayer said that Crane was within reaching distance of the top and approximately ten feet above his last screw when he stopped to place a final screw. As he was attempting to place the screw, he lost his left crampon placement when a piece of ice supporting the left foot popped off. His left tool placement then failed and he barn-doored out. Unable to recover, he then lost his right tool placement and fell upside down. His right crampon temporarily hung up and caused him a minor ankle injury prior to coming out.

He yelled while falling and never lost consciousness. He impacted the right side of his back against vertical ice of the upper column and came to a stop above the sloping ledge area. The belayer lowered him to the base of the route and began medical and rescue procedures with the aid of the other two ice climbers. Park personnel and volunteers responded to complete the rescue.

Analysis

Objective hazards are an integral part of ice climbing. Some hazards, such as breakage of ice holds and dislodging of loose ice, are routinely expected. Other hazards, such as the open spray of water at the top of a normally dry route, may be more of a surprise. The assessment of objective hazards and changing conditions is generally much more serious for an ice climbing leader than for a sport rock climb leader, hence the longer time that it generally takes for one to develop good lead ice climbing skills. Visual inspection of an ice route may or may not reveal all of the possible hazards. When the lead ice climber in this incident recognized that the water spray was becoming an obvious hazard, he had two choices: he could either lower off from his last placement after supplementing it with an additional ice screw (and then retrieve his gear on top-rope), or he could lead through the hazard. There is no right or wrong choice, but there are always possible negative consequences to either choice. Had he decided to lower off, his highest anchor may have failed before he could have supplemented it. The negative consequence of leading through was unfortunately the incident that occurred here. He made a reasonable choice and failed, but he may have just as easily succeeded had the ice supporting his left crampon not broken off. This is both the beauty and the ugliness inherent to ice climbing.

There were possible mitigating measures he could have chosen once he realized that his vision was impaired and he stopped to place an ice screw. First, when placing an ice screw, the leader should make absolutely sure that s/he has the best possible stance and tool placements. In this case, he was on the stance for some time before the ice failed, so the stance is not the most significant issue. Second, if a lead ice climber is making a placement due to some compromised situation, such as the fogged glasses, there are some things which can help with completing the placement. Possibilities that experienced ice climbers have employed upon finding themselves in a similar situation have been to: 1) keep a "panic piece" 17cm ice screw, well sharpened and silicone-oiled, closest to reach on the climber's rack (some climbers even have a piece just held on with Velcro that they can rip off the front of their rack); 2) catch a loop of rope over the top of a securely-planted ice ax as a temporary belay whereas the belayer could tighten up on the leader and allow for the placement of protection; 3) attach an ice tool to the harness of the leader with a fifi hook or carabiner to allow the leader to place protection; or 4) place a temporary fast piece of protection such as a spectre to allow the placement of a better piece. (Source: From a report submitted by Jim Detterline and Rich Perch, Park Rangers in Rocky Mountain National Park, and personal communication with local climbers)

FALL ON ROCK, CLIMBING ALONE AND UNROPED, NO HARD HAT, EXCEEDING ABILITIES
Colorado, Eldorado Canyon State Park, Redgarden Wall
On May 23, a male (22) was free-soloing the route Smoke and Mirrors, rated 5.10a, high on Redgarden Wall in Eldorado Canyon when several climbers witnessed his fall. He hit a ledge 40 feet down then fell another 60 feet before being wedged behind a flake on a small ledge several hundred feet above the ground. Another climber, who happened to be a paramedic, made his way to the victim quickly and called 911. The victim was marginally conscious with a head injury and had no feeling or movement below his waist. RMRG units arrived with medical kits and stabilized him with intravenous fluids, pain medication, and splinting. He was packaged and placed in a litter mid-wall. He required a 500-foot vertical evacuation to a gully, where a 800-foot scree evacuation to the valley floor was performed. He was then evacuated across South Boulder Creek via a Tyrolean traverse to a ground ambulance. The ambulance transported him down the canyon to an awaiting air ambulance, which flew him to the ER.
Analysis
If the fall had not been witnessed, the climber would have been virtually invisible. It is unknown whether his plans had been shared with anyone else. He was

exceedingly lucky to survive this accident in remote, highly technical terrain. (Source: From a report by the Rocky Mountain Rescue Group)

FALL ON SNOW—UNABLE TO SELF-ARREST, FAULTY USE OF CRAMPONS
Colorado, Indian Peaks Wilderness

On June 12, Mark Oveson (36) was traversing the snowfields between North Arapaho Peak and "Deshawa Peak" (point 12,800' on the USGS map) when he slipped. He tried to self-arrest, but lost his ice ax. He then tried to stop his slide with his feet. He was wearing crampons. One caught his leg, but he did not feel anything until he stood up at the end of his run. He had fractured his fibula and a bone in his ankle.

Analysis

Traversing across the top of the snowfield was tedious. At the time of my fall, I was wishing that we were at the bottom of the snowfield so that we could walk on relatively flat snow to our objective. I knew the runout was safe, so I was being careless in my steps. I should have either taken off my crampons and slid to the bottom or used caution to avoid falling. I now know that any fall while wearing crampons is serious.

Also, my ice ax was not tethered to my wrist. This was a careless oversight. If I had fallen where the runout was not safe, it could have been a tragic error. (Source: Mark Oveson)

RAPPEL/LOWERING FAILURE—FALL ON ROCK, NO HARD HAT
Colorado, Boulder Canyon

On June 22, two climbers were on a route behind Boulder Falls in Boulder Canyon. The leader, who had more than 20 years of rock climbing experience, topped out and placed an anchor. He was then lowered on that anchor by his belayer. While he was still 25 feet above the ground, the belayer lost control when the end of the rope ran through his belay device. The leader was dropped and sustained numerous injuries, including a serious head injury.

Analysis

The leader survived with a severe head injury. The two climbers reportedly had recently met and were doing their first climb together. The climbers under-estimated the length of the climb and over estimated the length of their rope. The belayer was not watching the end of the rope nor was there a safety knot tied to prevent the end from passing through. The leader was not wearing a helmet. (Source: From a report by the Rocky Mountain Rescue Group)

STRANDED, EXPOSURE—HYPOTHERMIA, INADEQUATE CLOTHING/ EQUIPMENT, CLIMBING ALONE, WEATHER, EXCEEDING ABILITIES
Colorado, Rocky Mountain National Park, Longs Peak

On September 4 at 0400, Sudheer Averineni (26) from Fort Collins began an attempt on Longs Peak with two other companions starting at the Longs Peak Trailhead. They had intended to complete their ascent within one day and were not equipped to stay out overnight. At 1030, the solo mountaineer separated from his group at the Keyhole Formation (13,100 feet above sea level), and continued on alone, in a snowstorm, towards the summit. Two mountaineers descending the Keyhole Route saw him at the base of the Homestretch, and later said that he did not appear to be in any difficulty.

The blizzard intensified with winds up to 60 mph, low temperatures to 5 degrees F, lightning, low visibility, and snow accumulations of up to six inches. The solo mountaineer's friends left the area and at 1627 reported him as missing/overdue to Rocky Mountain National Park Communications Center.

On September 5, a park ranger found his body on the summit of Longs Peak. He was lightly dressed in a hooded sweatshirt over a T-shirt, blue jeans, wool gloves, cotton socks, and sneakers. There was no extra clothing in his pack. He had a cell phone in the pocket of his sweatshirt, and although he may have attempted to call out, there was no record of his call with any of the surrounding 911 emergency communications centers. The cause of death was exposure.

Analysis

This fellow had unsuccessfully attempted Longs Peak via the Keyhole Route on two earlier occasions in 2004. In interviewing friends and mountaineers who had contact with him on the mountain, the investigator concluded that he apparently had a case of being goal oriented. He was inexperienced but apparently had great mental drive to get him to where he wanted to go. It is not known for certain why he did not attempt to descend.

He was inadequately clothed and equipped for winter conditions and a technical ascent. He failed to heed the advice of available literature and bulletins, friends, fellow mountaineers, and even park staff.

This was only the second year since the 1868 first-reported ascent of Longs Peak that the Keyhole Route was not rated as a non-technical hike at any time. Rangers had posted current peak conditions and weather forecasts at the Longs Peak Trailhead, advising of the "technical" conditions and the incoming blizzard. (Source: From a report submitted by Jim Detterline and Rich Perch, Park Rangers in Rocky Mountain National Park, and the *Rocky Mountain News*, September 8, 2004)

FALL ON ROCK—OFF ROUTE, DARKNESS
Colorado, Eldorado Canyon, Anthill Direct

On October 21, Angus McInnes (39) and his companion, a young Russian man (17) who had emigrated with his family to the U.S. four months earlier, were climbing Anthill Direct (5.9) when apparently they got off route.

McInnes was experienced, but he had not climbed the route previously. As daylight faded with the crux still ahead, McInnes started looking for a descent route. Instead of rappelling from their current anchor point, he decided to work left, perhaps in hope of gaining access to the easier route Red Guard in order to complete the climb.

The second lost sight of McInnes, who soon yelled, "Watch me." Shortly after, the second felt the leader pull lots of slack. Moments passed and then the rope came taut. The second radioed and yelled to McInnes but got no reply. The second did not know how to tie off the taut rope, so he began lowering the leader. After feeding several feet of rope, he felt his partner come to a stop. The second then removed the rope from his belay device, tied the rope off, and yelled for help.

Bystanders reported hearing cries for help from climbers 350 feet above the ground. RMRG was in the middle of another climbing rescue on the Flatirons to the north, but responded along with several other agencies. The second spoke limited English, which combined with darkness, slowed the rescue. Only when rescuers arrived at the position of the second did they find out about the predicament of the leader. Another rescuer rappelled 50 feet west and found the leader who was deceased. He was several feet down a gully with a hex from his gear sling caught in a crack. The gear sling was around his neck and positioned in a way that restricted his breathing. There was also a laceration under his helmet on the left side, but the coroner determined the cause of death was asphyxiation.

RMRG assisted the second off the cliff and evacuated the body of the leader that night, finishing at 0330 hours. It took a total of eight hours and required 45 rescuers from RMRG and several other agencies.

Analysis

The victims were climbing very late in the day and may have felt pressed by the rapidly fading light. By climbing off route, the lead climber entered unknown ground which quickly became very difficult. Sometimes it is better to continue with the plan you started with, or a safer bet may be to rappel. The lead climber was probably unconscious after his fall, thus could not respond to the second's attempt at communicating. Unable to communicate and with rapidly approaching darkness, the inexperienced second decided to lower McInnes. (Source: From a report by the Rocky Mountain Rescue Group)

(Editor's Note: Two other fatalities and one serious injury were a result of separate incidents at Boulder Canyon in October. This popular area is attracting scramblers. They see climbers and want to give it a try themselves.

There was a fatality on Snowmass Peak—14,092'—in June. The victim, Mark Golden, 32 , was probably trying to find a "shortcut" on the way down. He fell about 2,000 feet. This is normally a mountain one climbs by hiking on trails, as the rock is not good for climbing.)

FALL ON ROCK—HANDHOLD BROKE OFF
Kentucky and Tennesse, Big South Fork National River & Recreation Area

Shelly Buchanan (49) of Norris, Tennessee, was bouldering on the Twin Arches formation on the afternoon of November 11th when a handhold broke off from a rock causing her to fall in a horizontal position six feet to the ground. The impact fractured her pelvis in four places and caused bruising to her ribs. The caretaker of a nearby backcountry hostel reported the accident via cell phone and remained with Buchanan throughout the incident. Ranger/EMTs Jimmy Barna and Randy Scoggins, ranger/parkmedic Kevin Moses, and four volunteers from the park rescue team stabilized Buchanan, which included the administration of IV fluids and pain medication, and evacuated her via wheeled litter. A LifeStar Bell 430 helicopter took advantage of a five-minute window amidst deteriorating visibility and weather conditions to land and fly Buchanan to University of Tennessee Medical Center, where she was admitted in stable condition. (Source: Chief Ranger's Office)

Analysis

We don't get many reports from this area, so it is included to indicate that there are several climbing spots in this part of the south. This report was gleaned from the NPS Morning Report. (Source: Jed Williamson)

FALL ON ROCK, CLIMBING ALONE AND UNROPED
Maine, Camden, The Ramparts

I think of the accident described here as the case of the wet ladder. On March 17, my girlfriend's dog, Kaya, and I, Ryan J. Howes (22), went on a 1.0 mile hike to a local climbing area called "The Ramparts," in Camden, Maine. I have soloed here on many occasions. I know the climbs here well and have taught climbing as an Assistant Instructor for a college climbing class. My first climb of the day, called Natural History (5.7), was approximately 70 feet in length and was accomplished without difficulty to the rappel anchors. I rappelled off using a rope that I carried as a butterfly coil on my back while climbing.

The second climb was another story though! The Fireman's Ladder (5.6) is a corner that was wet in some areas because it had snowed the day before and the snow had melted. The thought did cross my mind that I was over confident, but I climbed anyway. As I approached the top at about 30 feet above the ground, I found myself on wet rock. I realized that I should down-climb and get off the climb. I now feel that continuing the climb would have ultimately kept me from writing this article.

While hanging off a hand jam in a wide crack, I turned 90 degrees away from the rock to wipe off my left foot with my left hand. During the rotation, the hand jam slipped and I continued to rotate free in the air and found myself facing outward while plunging down the vertical climb. After falling about ten feet, I saw that I was going to smash into the rock, but kicked myself away from it using my right leg and foot. I hit the ground and landed on both feet, but apparently my left leg and foot absorbed most of the impact of stopping. The fall continued until I was on both knees and then my hands and stomach. At first I was simply shocked from falling that distance, but then pain began to increase, so that within 15 or 20 seconds I knew that I was not walking out of the climbing area. There was approximately one and one-half hours of daylight left.

I took my helmet off and replaced it with a warm hat. The dog, Kaya, knew that I was hurt and she stayed by my side as I crawled the mile back to the trailhead through a talus field and over two streams. The crawl out took an hour, during which I kept calling for help and was in pain. At the Trailhead, next to the road, a number of cars drove past without stopping until I raised my hand for help and the first motorist screeched to a stop, laying down tire rubber in the process. Earlier, in crossing the streams, I stayed relatively dry, but near the Trailhead I had to crawl through standing water, was shivering, and started to go into shock. The motorist called 911 and an ambulance came and took me to Pennobscot Bay Medical Center, where I was treated for soft tissue tears and snapped ligaments in my left ankle and foot. A specialist has indicated that I will completely recover in a surprisingly short eight weeks. If true, this will be a small price to pay for such a mishap.

Analysis

A friend gave me a number of issues of Accidents in North American Mountaineering containing summaries of accidents in the USA over the last 40 to 50 years. I found that my situation fit many of the leading causes or relationships to accidents, including my age group (21-25), moderate experience level, falling or slipping on rock, and climbing unroped, among others.

I now realized that soloing is very unpredictable, particularly when coupled with poor judgment. I have decided to climb with a partner or use a mechanical soloist device. Maybe my new decision to climb roped up and with a partner will keep me old, but perhaps not as bold.

(Editor's Note: Self reports are the best! There was one other climbing-related accident in Maine this year, gleaned from the NPS Morning Report, though not counted in the data. Emil Lin, 21, of Hampden, Maine, drowned while attempting to retrieve a climbing shoe from the ocean below Otter Cliffs, one of the most popular local climbing destinations, which can be extremely treacherous during stormy weather and high tides. Lin had been at the base of the cliff when surf from the high tide washed his gear out into the water. Although the gear was attached to his climbing rope, his shoe came off and started floating away. Lin entered the 49-degree F water to retrieve it, only to be overpowered by both the cold water and high surf. After several attempts to climb back up onto the rocks, Lin went under and did not resurface.)

FALL ON ROCK, HANDHOLD BROKE OFF, INADEQUATE PROTECTION
Missouri, Henley Wall

Dave Ogrodowczyk (age unknown) was climbing at the Henley Wall in Henley, Missouri with two of his students and another friend. Both Dave and his belayer were wearing helmets during the incident. The belayer was secured to a tree with and adequate anchor. There was no extra slack in the rope.

Dave was attempting a climb called "Blackbeard," a 5.9 mixed route. The route headed up the cliff to a ledge (easy climbing, protection poor), proceeded up a steep face (5.9 climbing, 4 bolts), then finished up a relatively easy face with pretty good protection.

Dave climbed up to the first ledge and clipped the first bolt easily. He continued up the steep face clipping the next three bolts. A little further up, he placed a #1 Camalot. He climbed another 15 feet. Here, he opted not to place another piece (placement was poor) as he needed to make only one more relatively easy move before clipping into the chain anchor.

The move required Dave to mantel a small shelf. He located a possible hand hold, gave it a tug, and determined it was strong enough to support his weight. Just as he committed to making the move, however, the rock broke from the cliff and went tumbling down. Dave fell about 30 feet. As he stopped at the end of the rope, he impacted the cliff with his left foot.

The belayer lowered him to the ground. His left ankle was swollen and treated with ice. Further x-rays revealed that Dave had fractured his medial malleolus (inner ankle) bone.

Analysis

It is possible that Dave could have placed another piece of protection before committing to the final move of the climb, but this does not ensure that he would not have gotten hurt. The place for protection was marginal for taking a piece of gear.

Dave believes that the real cause of injury was attributed to a previous injury in which his left leg was surgically repaired with a tibial rod and screws. When he impacted the cliff, it was his left foot that took the force. The force was applied to his ankle where the screws affixed the tibial rod. His ankle broke in just this spot. (Source: Local climber, name unknown)

FALL ON ROCK, EXPOSURE, DARKNESS
Nevada, Red Rocks Canyon, Epinephrine

On October 30, climbers Joel Geerling (24) and Chris Pannucci (25) left the Black Velvet Canyon parking lot at 0530, arriving at the base of 18-pitch Epinephrine (5.9) by 0630. The pair had previously climbed Crimson Chrysalis (9-pitch, 5.8+) and Dream of Wild Turkeys (7-pitch, 5.10-) at Red Rocks in March of 2003. They planned a one-day ascent of Epinephrine and did not bring a second rope or bivy gear outside of two emergency space blankets. After struggling through the lower chimney sections they began linking pitches and arrived at the bolt anchor of pitch 17 with 60 minutes of daylight left. Geerling pulled a small bulge above the anchors to a ledge, placed a tri-cam, and began traversing into the final dihedral. During the traverse, a handhold pulled from the sandstone and he barn-doored into the opposite wall. He fell ten feet and sustained blunt trauma to his right knee. A local guide on the route immediately below the pair passed Pannucci and provided first aid to Geerling's knee; he and his climber planned to wait for the pair at the summit. Pannucci led pitch 18 and brought Geerling to his stance as darkness fell. Given Geerling's injury, the two decided to remain roped for the 700 feet of fourth-class terrain to the summit. Pannucci led 200 feet and built an anchor. As he ascended, Geerling (a 5.12 climber) fell once on the fourth class terrain and arrived at the belay ledge shivering, disoriented and in severe pain, his leg nearly locked in the straightened position as it swelled. The pair considered bivying and completing the climb in the morning but Pannucci was unsure of Geerling's ability to make the extensive descent from Whiskey Peak. From the summit, the guide used his cellular phone to activate the Las Vegas Search and Rescue and rappelled to the pair's ledge until their location was identified by helicopter. Geerling was man-winched to the summit and evacuated by helicopter to a waiting ambulance. He was treated at the UMC Trauma Center for hypothermia (93 F), evaluated for a fractured patella, and received stitches for his knee laceration.

Analysis

Loose rock is common even on often-climbed routes in this area. Rain two days prior to the incident may have contributed to the hold breaking.

In the interest of speed, the pair had brought minimal gear and were unprepared for anything but an emergency bivy. They also did not have a second rope, so an up-and-over ascent was their only option.

On the fourth class terrain, Geerling exhibited classic signs of hypothermia (loss of coordination, disorientation, mental slowing), likely brought on by the combined effect of injury, exposure, and exhaustion. The pair's position on a ledge several hundred feet below the summit slowed Geerling's rescue as a search and rescue team had to be airlifted to the summit to create a man-winch. (Source: Chris Pannucci and Joel Geerling, the climbers.)

FALL ON SNOW/ICE, FAULTY USE OF CRAMPONS, INADEQUATE EQUIPMENT, INEXPERIENCE
New Hampshire, Mount Washington, Pipeline Gully

On March 9, Robert Douglas (39), John Corse (38), and Colin O'Farrell (23) became involved in a situation requiring climbing techniques due to the conditions they found when they attempted to find a good backcountry ski descent route on the west side of Mount Washington. Colin O'Farrell provided this description:

I met John and Rob at the Cog Railway base station. I had never skied with either of them, but had numerous conversations with Rob regarding backcountry skiing in the White and Green Mountains. We skinned up alongside the Cog Railway and then worked our way north along the Gulfside Trail looking for good snow. It had rained with a changeover to snow a few days before, consequently there was both fresh snow and icy hard-pack. Rob had been having difficulty keeping his crampons on, so we stopped, pulled out a Leatherman, and he readjusted them.

We found a gully off of Mount Clay that looked promising. We skied the upper 1/3-1/2 in about six inches of snow. We stopped at the transition to hard-pack and decided to head back up in order to either lap the upper portion again or find another gully. In transitioning from skis to crampons, John Corse lost his footing and fell the length of the gully, coming to rest on the apron below. Rob and I heard his cries for help. I immediately began descending with crampons and ice ax, while Rob elected to sidestep/side-slip his way down on skis. I asked him to give me a lot of distance so as to avoid any complications. I reached John and found him conscious and oriented but in a lot of pain and with facial trauma. At the time I thought his chief issues were ribs and tib/fib. Rob reached the top of the icefall that [as a result of] the low snow year of 03/04 separated the gully proper from the apron below. I advised Rob to throw his backpack/skis down to us and descend the mellowest part of the ice, along climber's left. Rob did not have an ice ax, so he was holding his ski poles near the baskets in an attempt to gain additional purchase on the ice.

About halfway down, Rob lost a crampon. From my vantage point, it looked like he decided to jump and aim for a pocket of windslab at the base of the ice in the hopes that he would arrest his fall. It was perhaps an eight to ten foot jump. He failed to arrest his fall, gathered speed and slid through the boulder field in which John and I were sitting. He came to rest slightly above John and me.

He had no breath or pulse, so I commenced CPR for 30 minutes, but to no avail. At this time I put in the 911 call and asked for a helicopter. I ceased CPR on Rob and focused on keeping John warm, comfortable, and awake. The rescuers from the Mount Washington Observatory reached us shortly after sundown and put the call in for the heli. Given our location on the side-slope of the ravine, we had to move John to a better pick up point, using a Sked litter. John was lifted into the helicopter and I opted to get a ride with him as well. We landed at the Glen and were transferred the hospital in Berlin via ambulance.

Analysis

I spoke with Colin O'Farrell and some individuals from Mountain Rescue Service (the North Conway based team). All agreed that in addition to skiing ability, mountaineering skills and equipment are required in this kind of terrain. Many backcountry skiers, if not carrying ice axes, use ski poles with picks fixed just below the handles for self-arrest purposes. Setting up an anchor and/or creating a platform when switching from skis to crampons in technical terrain, especially where a fall is possible, are common practices. On this day and in this gully, conditions required good skiing ability and winter mountaineering skills, along with the appropriate equipment for same. John Corse, an avid backcountry skier who had negotiated many good ski routes in the White and Green Mountains, did not have the equipment or mountaineering skills required for the terrain he and his partners encountered. (Source: From a report by Colin O'Farrell and Jed Williamson)

FAILURE TO TURN BACK, FAILURE TO FOLLOW ROUTE, INADEQUATE CLOTHING AND EQUIPMENT, WEATHER
New Hampshire, Mount Lafayette

Russel and Brenda Cox went for a hike to the summit of Mt. Lafayette early Sunday morning, March 21. They had planned to follow the Bridle Path and return the same way, often a ten hour round trip. They started hiking around 8:30 a.m. and reached the Greenleaf Hut, just at timberline, around 11:00 a.m. There they met a party who had been on the summit. They advised the couple that the weather was deteriorating and suggested that they turn around. The Coxes decided to continue to the summit. When they started down, they got lost in the worsening conditions, heading down the wrong trail. By the time they realized their error, they were in a whiteout with winds gusting to 75 mph. They had no clothing or gear for a night out. They built a snow cave and hunkered down. When they awoke on Monday, the weather had not improved.

When they didn't return by Monday morning, their son called authorities. Their car was found in the Falling Waters parking lot on Monday. Rescuers were called out but were unable to find the couple's tracks due to a very large snowfall the previous night. Conditions on Monday deteriorated, and around midnight the rescue was suspended.

Monday morning the Coxes continued on the trail, but by this time they and their clothing were wet. Unable to continue or to find their snow cave, they huddled together in a niche between several rocks. Sometime during the night, Mrs. Cox slipped into hypothermia and died.

The rescue resumed on Tuesday morning. The weather had dramatically improved, allowing for the use of a N.H. National Guard Blackhawk helicopter. Members of the local Mountain Rescue Service were ferried to the top of the ridge and started searching at the same time as volunteers started up the surrounding trails. Sometime in mid-morning Mr. Cox crawled from his niche and spotted the helicopter and managed to attract its attention. Mr. Cox and his wife's body were airlifted out.

Analysis

The Franconia Notch area is known for its volatile weather, especially above timberline, and it was known that a large storm was on its way.

Mountain Rescue Service President Rick Wilcox pointed out that most of their rescues are the result of the following issues or some combination thereof: The party 1) started late; 2) didn't check the weather; 3) were unprepared to stay out—no bivouac gear; 4) had no preset turnaround time—i.e. pressed on when they should have retreated; 5) had little or no knowledge of the descent route; and 6) exceeded their abilities.

Incidents like this, while not entered in the data because they are not climbing accidents, are reported because they illustrate how a hiking situation can turn into the need for mountaineering skills. (Source: Edited from a report by Al Hospers)

FALLING ROCK—FALL ON ROCK
New Hampshire, Cannon Cliff, Whitney-Gilman

May 18 was a gorgeous day when two former students of mine and I headed up on the Whitney-Gilman ridge about 10:00 a.m. after waiting for one party of three to advance the first two pitches. I led the first pitch and brought J.W. and P.G. up simultaneously, as we were climbing with a double rope system. Our plan was to swing leads and enjoy the route and not worry about rushing the climb having committed to climbing below another party.

P.G. topped the second pitch out and discovered that two of the party of three were still on the small belay stance/ledge, so he anchored below and waited patiently for them to move upwards. After the belay station was clear, he constructed a new anchor and brought us up.

As we all gathered on the ledge, the first party of three had a problem with a piece of protection becoming stuck in the crack on the third pitch. After the followers gave up, the leader rappelled with three nut tools duct taped together to give it go in removing the camming unit. This whole process went on for almost two hours. Needless to say, we were getting a bit impatient with the whole process, so we decided to do the left hand variation. After identifying the route from the belay ledge, J.W. began the pitch. After ten meters he began to climb out and left. P.G. and I encouraged J.W. to stay right, on the route we identified. J.W. responded that the pins going left looked good, as did the climbing. I said, "All right, just let us know how it looks around the corner." J.W. said, " The climbing looks easy, no problem."

Meanwhile another party of two were topping out on the first pitch. A few minutes latter we heard some rock fall. Shortly after that we heard a blood curdling "AAHHHHH!!" Almost simultaneously, we heard another rock fall. We hear J.W. moaning and yelling, having hit a ledge after about an eight to ten meter fall. While climbing on double ropes, the upper blue rope's protection (small stopper) pulled out of the rock causing him to fall until the second green rope came taut just has he hit the ledge. The sheath of the blue rope was cut all the way through and there was visual damage on the core strands about three meters in from end.

I jumped into rescue mode and ascended the pitch using a friction wrap for running pro on the tight green rope. Being extra careful to assure not falling on this rope, I aided over the awkward move into the corner and ledge where J.W. was. After a full patient assessment, I determined he possibly had broken ribs, a back injury, and a sprained ankle. Knowing we weren't dealing with an airway, head injury, c-spine injury or any signs of internal bleeding, we decided it was best to facilitate the rescue ourselves.

I was able to climb a few meters above J.W. and established an anchor. Meantime P.G. was reworking the last belay anchor to facilitate a lower and a rappel. As J.W. was able to stand fairly balanced and ambulatory (but in intense pain), I was able to lower him to the belay stance where P.G. was able to anchor him and get him in position of comfort. I removed a couple of pieces from the anchor and rappelled down to a belay stance for further assessment.

The next section I needed to lower P.G. on two ropes in order for him to set two directional anchors during his descent. When he arrived at the final ledge, he began constructing the next lower/rappel anchor. I then simul-rappelled with J.W., positioning him sitting on my thigh keeping him upright with a chest sling clipped into a rappel extension material utilizing a prusik for an auto-locking back up. I was able to pass my directional points with good stances providing enough security to clip uphill strand into directional carabiner and downhill strands out. Once I reached the new anchor and ledge, P.G. anchored and positioned J.W. while I jugged/Bat-manned up rappel strands on friction wrap to free one directional anchor and pull knot past top directional anchor and rapped back to ledge to pull the ropes.

Our last section I lowered P.G. to ensure the strands made it down clean and simul-rappelled into the Black Dike with J.W.. We touched down on the talus field three hours after the initial accident. It took another two hours for J.W. to move backwards (his only real position of comfort) while leaning his chest on a tight short rope supported by me uphill and had his feet being assisted and guided by P.G. on the downhill side. Half way down the scree/talus we witnessed a very large rockfall come down to the left, about 100-150 meters of the Whitney/Gilman and all the way down the talus field to our south. It was quite the exclamation point on our day.

Once on the paved walkway, I was able to fireman carry J.W. to the truck where we transported him to the hospital. We never heard a word from either party, above or below. J.W. spent the next two nights in hospital. He had two vertebrae compression fractures and a strained ankle and was very happy there wasn't anything worse! (Source: From a letter sent in by Mark Puleio, mountain guide.)

(Editor's Note: Cannon Cliff is the rock formation where the New Hampshire State symbol USED to be. The famous stone profile known as the Old Man of the Mountains exfoliated last summer. Spontaneous rockfall is a common phenomenon and one of the inherent risks for climbers.)

FALL ON ROCK, PROTECTION FAILED
New York, Shawangunks, Boston

On November 6, a climber (53) fell about 30 feet from the crux of Boston (5.4+ or 5.5, PG). A cam placed two or three feet below the point from which he fell failed (broke). The next pro was at about 15 feet and was too low to keep him off the ground.

He had placed two pieces of protection at ten to 15 feet (at "the triangle"). He and the group spoke about that being the last good place to put in gear before the off-width and that a ground fall was a serious concern past that point. He then climbed the off-width and into the good stance below the crux. He placed the cam below the crux, started to climb into the crux, reversed to the comfortable stance, and extended the cam with a runner. He was struggling with the crux, and a partner provided some beta based on his having climbed the route recently, so he switched to a lieback, still struggled, then fell. He hit the ground on a loose rope.

His climbing partners and two EMTs who were on a nearby climb gave assistance immediately. He was put on a stretcher and evacuated quickly and taken by ambulance to St. Francis Trauma Center. He was unconscious though breathing when he arrived at the hospital, but died without regaining consciousness three days later.

Analysis

I think there are two main points to be learned about cams from this accident. First, the degradation of performance of all cams in a placement such as this—in an uneven, nubbly crack in hard rock—is probably much greater than most climbers believe. Second, this is especially true of cams made of die cast aluminum because the material is weaker to begin with and much more brittle. I don't think any manufacturers in the U.S. or western Europe currently manufacture cams of die cast aluminum, but there are still lots of them around on climbers' racks. Climbers should probably get rid of them, or at least be aware that they are much less forgiving of non-standard placements than are modern cams made of 7075 or other similarly strong and ductile aluminum.

Someone would do the climbing community a favor by documenting the breaking strength of four-cam units when only two cams on the same side are holding. This would be a "standard, non-standard" test. (Source: Mark Nord)

VARIOUS FALLS ON ROCK, PROTECTION PULLING, FALLING ROCK, INADEQUATE PROTECTION
New York, Shawangunks

In addition to the above accident in the Gunks, there were 24 other reports, of which 17 are counted as climbing for purposes of this journal. Fourteen involved leader falls, and eight of those were the result of inadequate protection. Several of the falls occurred just after starting from the ground. Three injuries resulted from bouldering falls. There were a few incidents that resulted in inuries from falling rock as well. The average age of the climbers directly involved was 35, and most of the routes were of moderate difficulty. (Source: From reports submitted by the Mohonk Preserve)

LIGHTNING
North Carolina, Linville Gorge Wilderness, The Amphitheater, Daddy

In August, a party of two were climbing the Daddy (5.6) a classic 5-pitch route located in the Amphitheater, Linville Gorge Wilderness Area. The incident started when the lead climber (LC) was 65 feet above the large traverse ledge located on the third pitch of the route, when he suddenly found himself unable to climb upwards (he was climbing on double ropes). He yelled to his belayer (B) who was positioned on the ledge, with no response. LC then yanked on the rope to get B's attention, again without response. LC looked down and saw B lying face down on the ledge. LC rapped down, and found B regaining consciousness with blood on his face. His head was ok as he was wearing a helmet. LC secured his partner and with 70m of additional rope rappelled to the ground and made his way to the trailhead for help. On his way out, LC ran into climbers Gary and Carol on the Jonas Ridge trail. Carol left the area to call for assistance. Both the North Carolina Outward Bound School and Burke County EMS responded.

In the meantime, LC and Gary walked to a position on the rim of the Amphitheater almost directly across from the route Daddy, where Gary was able to make brief verbal contact with B. After making contact with B, both LC and Gary traversed east around the top of the Amphitheater in worsening weather (by now it was raining hard) to the top of Daddy. Gary rappelled down to the ledge to assist B only to find him gone! All that remained on the ledge was the belay anchor high in the crack and a cut rope. Gary ascended his rope back to the top of the climb.

Because of the heavy rain, B became concerned about hypothermia and took matters into his own hands; he rappelled to the ground and climbed the fourth class descent gully out of the Amphitheater where he was eventually met by a member of the hasty team. He was able to walk out of the area unassisted.

After two CAT scans and retrospectively putting the clues together, B believes that he was struck by lightning. In trying to piece together the incident, he remembered that one of his shoes had been blown off his foot.

He also had a blistered left foot, blackened toes, and remembers hearing a "popping" sound before going into unconsciousness. He said, "Last time I heard that sound, I was close to a lightning strike."

Analysis

After putting the clues together, B hypothesized that he was zapped by what a friend described as a phenomena known as "ball" lighting. It apparently exhibits buzzing sounds but no flash and precedes storms. Late day thunderstorms are a common summer occurrence in North Carolina. Climbers can prepare themselves by getting an early start and recognizing the signs of a potential thunderstorm. Familiarization with the appropriate tactics and techniques to help mitigate potential lightning strike will also be helpful.

During the quick hike to the top of the route, I (Gary) began thinking that many of my partners and my own self-rescue skills have become rusty or lost due to disuse. I urge all traditional climbers to learn, practice, and keep these skills current. As climbers, we should be capable of rescuing ourselves or other climbers and not rely solely on local rescue services. The North Carolina Outward Bound School, however, is consistently competent and should always be contacted in the Linville Gorge area as they are one of the primary SAR groups in the vicinity. Their support that day is appreciated, as is the quick response of the Burke Co. EMS. (Source: Gary Butler, from a posting on the Carolina Climbers Coalition Website www.carolinaclimbers.org, August 13, 2004, Kristian Jackson, NCOBS, and Aram Attarian).

FALL OR SLIP ON ROCK, EXCEEDING ABILITIES
North Carolina, Pilot Mountain State Park

On September 5, Paul Bridges (PB) and Alex Rodriguez (AR) were rappelling in Pilot Mountain State Park, which is located approximately 25 miles north of Winston Salem. After both had rappelled several times during the morning, they decided to do a little "climbing." Leaving their rappelling equipment behind, they moved down the trail to the base of the climbing area and began to free-solo an unknown route. As AR was attempting to move up onto a ledge, he lost his grip and fell a few feet to a ledge below injuring his ankles. After hitting this ledge, he tumbled down the rockface to the trail below, receiving additional injuries. PB believes AR fell approximately 12 to 15 feet.

Pilot Knob Fire Department, Pilot Mountain Rescue Squad, Surry County EMS and the Interagency High Angle Rescue Team all responded. AR was placed in a Stokes basket and hauled up the main descent gully. He was carried out and transported to the hospital, where his injuries were evaluated. He sustained two broken ankles, a fractured right tibia and fibula, broken and dislocated fingers and torn tendons on his left hand. He also cracked ribs and several stitches were required to close a head wound! As of September 10, AR has undergone several surgeries, and still awaiting more.

Analysis

Some of the terrain at Pilot Mountain looks relatively easy and for some presents the path of least resistance to the top of the climbing area. Both climbers had the equipment to set up a top-roped climb. Whether or not they had the knowledge is another story. (Source: Keith D. Martin, Pilot Mountain State Park Ranger and Aram Attarian)

FALL OR SLIP ON ROCK, PROTECTION PULLED OUT, FAILURE TO FOLLOW INSTINCTS
North Carolina, Table Rock, Talkin' 'Bout Mudflaps

During the morning of October 17, Jeff Pock (36) fell while climbing Talkin' 'Bout Mudflaps (5.11) causing his first piece of protection, a #3 stopper, to pull, resulting in a ground fall. He suffered two broken heels, a broken left foot and a broken left wrist.

Jeff mentioned that he and his partner and their girlfriends were on their way to climb Second Stanza (5.8). Jeff was leading the group to the start of the climb. He stopped beneath Talkin' 'Bout Mud Flaps to wait for his party to catch up. After arriving, his partner suggested that they climb Talkin' 'Bout Mud Flaps instead of continuing to Second Stanza, their intended climb. Jeff reluctantly agreed. Later, he commented that he had a bad feeling about the route and that he didn't feel comfortable with his decision, as he had a very limited amount of lead climbing experience, especially at this level of difficulty.

Jeff recalled starting the climb and missing clipping the first fixed anchor. He continued upwards and placed a stopper and in the process of placing a cam to backup the stopper he lost his footing and began to fall, the stopper popped. He remembers the sensation of being in mid-air, then striking the ledge below with his heels and doing a clean flip before hitting the ground. Joe mentioned that when the stopper popped, "It was the sickest sound I've ever heard."

Chris Rhyne and his partner who were climbing nearby, were first on the scene and with the help of Joe's party were able to evacuate him using a piggyback carry. This was a difficult task, as the terrain and narrow climbers trail proved to be very demanding. After reaching the main Table Rock (TR) trail, the rescuers were able to do a two-person carry down to the TR parking lot and their vehicle. Joe was driven to Sloop Memorial Hospital in Crossnore, N.C., approximately one hour away where his injuries were assessed.

Analysis

Overall the climbers, with assistance, were able to initiate a self-rescue. The ability to be self-sufficient is a skill set that all climbers should have. Intuition is something that many of us, including climbers, possess. When intuition tells you that something doesn't feel right, heed its warning! (Source: Chris Rhyne, Joe Pock and Aram Attarian)

FALL ON SNOW, INADEQUATE PROTECTION, INADEQUATE BELAY
Oregon, Mount Hood, Castle Crags

On April 3, Doug Adair (50) and Debra Marsh (47) attempted to climb a variation on Castle Crags, a steep buttress separating the south and west sides of Mount Hood. They proceeded from Illumination Saddle up snow ramps which became progressively steeper. Doug climbed up to the first obvious notch in the crater rim to get a view, then down-climbed back to Debra. He proceeded to traverse approximately 100 feet below the crater rim towards Reid Headwall, in search of a way to reach lower-angle slopes and eventually the summit ridge. This traverse proved quite difficult and time-consuming. Doug eventually encountered a fluting of extremely soft "bottomless" snow. After working his way across, he climbed up about 30 feet and waited for Debra to cross. He could not proceed farther and maintain a solid position due to large amounts of rime and a section of rock above. Doug planted both tools and feet, and placed a picket. He found fairly solid snow, but it was shallow (his picket hit rock at first). Doug estimates the slope angle was approximately 65 degrees at the traverse.

Debra slipped a bit on her first attempt to cross the loose snow, then fell. The force of the fall pulled Doug out of his stance and his picket out of the snow. The resulting fall was a tumbling, 1,000-foot ride over several cliffs and gullies, including the Reid Glacier bergschrund, to a stopping point at the head of the Reid Glacier. The fall resulted in fractures, abrasions, and lacerations to each climber.

Analysis

Protection can be difficult to come by on the steeper climbs on Mount Hood. Rime ice and loose snow often require innovative and unorthodox techniques to get an adequate belay. Sometimes belays are simply inadequate, no matter the skill or experience the climber may have. While the climbers reported good conditions early in the climb, other experienced climbers the previous day encountered unconsolidated "sugar" under a weak crust in the immediate vicinity of the accident. Often, it *may* be safer to continue unroped to avoid pulling the entire team off in the event of a fall or simply back off the climb altogether if possible. Climbing roped with poor anchors can provide a false sense of security. In these cases, the rope may only ensure that "no man falls alone."

The "belay" did not involve pulling in rope as the follower traversed. This resulted in approximately five feet of slack in the rope, which allowed the follower to pick up speed before the belay took the force of the fall. When protection is marginal, every attempt should be made to minimize forces on that protection. A more formal belay may have been more appropriate in these challenging conditions.

The climbing party encountered very difficult traversing at the elevation they chose. It took much longer than they had expected, and the fall occurred after 1100. It is recommended to be off steep snow and ice as early as possible to avoid any sun influenced instability, though the snow the party encountered appeared to be part of a longer-term trend in conditions.

After the fall, both climbers mistakenly thought the other had a phone in their pack. Without a phone, it was luck alone that a member of Portland Mountain Rescue happened to stop over at the saddle to check conditions on the Reid Glacier as he was skiing down from the summit. People rarely travel on the Reid late in the day, and the immobilized party could have been there for a very long time.

Though helicopters were requested and succeeded in evacuating the patients, whiteout conditions hampered air rescue attempts for a short time. Climbers encountering an accident must be aware that helicopter rescue is not always possible or appropriate. Even if a helicopter is available to assist, contingency plans should always be made. (Source: Iain Morris, Portland Mountain Rescue)

FALL ON SNOW—FAULTY USE OF CRAMPONS
Oregon, Mount Jefferson

On Sunday morning, April 25, Brent McGregor (51) and Tom Herron (40) began a climb of Mount Jefferson. McGregor and his climbing partner had started their climb at 3:00 a.m. Sunday but did not reach the summit until around 5:30 p.m., as heavy, wet spring snow challenged their every step. "The snow was pretty soggy, and we had a late summit – later than we should have," he recalled. "The snow conditions slowed us way down."

The pair were ankle and sometimes knee-deep in snow on their journey. "Once you stepped onto the crust layer, you're way down to your ankles," he said. "It's very tiring, a long haul to the top. The snow was warm, and the freezing level was 11,000 feet, higher than the 10,495-foot peak.

McGregor summited the peak after fourteen hours of climbing as Herron, who was very tired, waited below. "We knew that we were going to have soft snow," he said, and as for the descent, "A lot of people say that's where you get hurt. My energy level was high. We knew we had two hours to get down the mountain that we would be able to use our headlamps to follow the (Pacific Crest Trail) out.

"We would have been fine, if I didn't slip," McGregor recounted. "I was going down maybe a 45-degree slope. The snow was really soft, and we were plunge-stepping down the mountain. (They were not roped together.)

"I hit an area where there was a sheet of ice, with two inches of fresh snow on top of it, instead of the deeper snow we were going on," he said. "The area around me, the surface snow broke loose. Everything came down and took me with it. I was face down to self-arrest...

"When I did that, it ripped through the snow," McGregor said. "I worked up a pretty fast speed for 15 to 20 feet. Then one of my crampon points hit the snow, and they caught. They say never wear crampons if you're going to glissade.

"Then I heard a snap, a pop," he said, of his fibula, down by the ankle. "I went a few more feet and stopped, because my other foot was buried under the snow. Similar to the friction of an avalanche, it built up a hard substance around my leg." Once he dug out his other foot with the ice ax, McGregor said, he saw "that (left) boot had been twisted completely around. It looked like it should have been broke, but it wasn't." Herron, who got within 100 feet of the summit Sunday, did not see McGregor fall, as he was on the other side of some rocks at that point in their descent.

"As soon as I stopped myself, that's when the pain hits real hard," McGregor recalled. "I sort of focus on breathing, calm myself down, try to collect my thoughts, wiggle my toes a little, bend my ankle, then I feel the pain. I called for (Herron), he came over, and I said, 'I'm not walking out.'"

Emergency dispatchers got a call on McGregor's cell phone around 7:30 p.m. but somehow got the mistaken impression the pair were closer to Pamelia Lake, a popular fishing and hiking area, according to Linn County Sheriff Dave Burright. Information that came in during the night made it clear that the pair were higher up the slope than earlier believed, at about 7,900 feet, the sheriff said.

"So we burrowed in and stayed there," McGregor said. "Tom used the ice ax and dug kind of like a small snow cave, wind break. We took the climbing rope and put it on my back, for insulation from the snow, took the foam pad out of the backpack, put all our clothes on, and looked up at the stars and down at the rescue lights.

Linn County Sheriff's Search and Rescue called for military helicopter assistance because of the danger and difficulty. The climbers were lifted off the mountain at mid-morning on the next day. After an hour at the emergency room, McGregor was released with a temporary cast. (Source: Robert Speik)

Analysis

Neither my partner nor I felt comfortable dropping down the mountain without our crampons on. There were icy areas we crossed that would have been very difficult to navigate without crampons. Common knowledge states plunge stepping with crampons should not be done. It was equally impractical to install and remove crampons to suit the snow and ice conditions. We felt we needed them for the icy sections, realizing they were less than ideal in the soft snow. We saw no perfect answer at the time.

Here are two things I could have done: 1) Turned and faced the mountain to down-climb the icy sections we encountered; or 2) find another route down the mountain. (Source: Brent McGregor)

FALL ON SNOW—UNABLE TO SELF-ARREST
Oregon, Mount Hood, South Side

After successfully ascending South Side on July 23, Zach Usadi-Henrickson (20) slipped on a steep section of snow roughly below the "Mazama Chute" as he was descending. He was unable to arrest the fall and came to rest just above the fumaroles (steam and sulfur vents) on the west side of the Hogsback at about 10:00 a.m. Usadi-Henrickson's two climbing partners helped stabilize his injuries and called for a rescue.

Analysis

The Cascade Volcanoes are notorious for rotten rock. Climbers usually only climb the steeper technical routes when the freezing level is low and the rock is secured by layers of rime ice. Generally speaking, by early July, most of the ice on the upper mountain has melted away, significantly increasing the risk of rockfall. Additionally, the bergshrund crevasses on the south side of Mount Hood have usually grown to the point that the are a much more formidable hazard then they are during the "normal" climbing season (May-June.)

These individuals chose to climb Mount Hood on the hottest day of the year, with temperatures predicted to be near 100 degrees in Portland and a 14 to 15,000 foot freezing level. According to the climbers, the snow conditions were good at the time of the accident and did not contribute to the accident, though there was significant rockfall that presented its own risks and endangered the patient once he came to rest after the fall. This was the patient's first technical climb, and he may not have been aware of the risks they were taking and the normal protocols for climbing this mountain.

To avoid accidents like this, climbers should: 1) Climb early and during periods when the rotten rock is relatively secure with rime ice; 2) climb with experienced partners who have good judgment, know proper techniques and protocols, and have the proper equipment; 3) research climbs to understand what normal procedures are for the intended route, and any extraordinary risks that may exist; and 4) check condition reports to understand what recent observations may exist.

All three climbers in this party were certified Wilderness First Responders. This training clearly paid off as the patient's two climbing partners did an excellent job of assessing and treating injuries. However, this was one of the classic dilemmas where a patient presented with possible spinal injuries that would indicate that they not be moved, but the extreme risk of rockfall necessitated moving the patient to protect him and the rescuers from more serious injuries. Nevertheless, the party is to be commended for their patient assessment and treatment of injuries, as well as their cooperation with rescuers and helping in the difficult rescue effort. They did very well given the conditions they encountered. (Source: Steve Rollins, Portland Mountain Rescue, and various newspaper reports)

FALL ON ROCK—HANDHOLD CAME OFF, FAILURE TO FOLLOW ROUTE
Oregon, Mount Washington, West Face

JWS (40) and I (BC, 42) attempted the West Face route on Mount Washington on August 21. It is rated a 5.6 in Jeff Thomas' guide *Oregon High*.

We are average climbers, 5.6/5.7 trad and 5.9 sport. We have done several multi-pitch routes—alpine and in climbing areas.

We climbed the peak a few weeks before (standard route) led by my wife so we could walk around the other side to scope out the route. We then attempted it two weeks later. It started raining lightly while we gained the ridge. While it was probably dry enough to climb, we turned around thinking we needed/wanted perfect conditions to climb this route.

Our next attempt was the following weekend. We left the van at 4:30 a.m. and started climbing at 9:00 a.m. JWS led the first pitch over fractured blocks and set up a bomber belay where we saw other slings and an old pin. I followed and started out on the second pitch. I went up and around a small corner. The rock seemed incredibly loose. Even more loose than the Southeast Spur that we climbed the year before.

I put in three pieces (cams). My last piece (#1 Camelot) was in a horizontal crack/flake. I climbed about seven or eight feet above it. The rock seemed even worse here. I was pulling over a slight bulge when the rock I committed to came off in my left hand. I fell approximately seven or eight feet striking my left foot on the small ledge where my last piece was located. I think, I then flipped backwards and fell another 7 or 8 feet before JWS caught the fall. This was at 10:15 a.m. (Note: after talking with someone who has climbed this route twice, I may have been off route.)

At that point, I was probably only ten to 15 feet above her but out of sight. JWS then lowered me slowly while I used my right foot and left knee to traverse down and over to her. As I got closer to her, she threw me two four-foot slings tied together so I was on two belays now (in case the piece that was holding my fall failed). From what I could tell, all three pieces held.

I reached JWS at 10:30 a.m. She tied me in and I sat down on a block just slightly below her where I used my cell phone and called the two friends who knew where/what we were doing. I alerted DK of the situation who then promptly called the Sheriff's office. I untied, JWS pulled the rope and then retied into my harness. JWS then slowly lowered me down while I used my right leg. At the steeper sections I sort of slid on my side/butt. After I reached the scree, JWS cleaned up the belay station and rapped down.

On the scree field, we stopped and made a plan. Fearing shock, I wanted to get in the sun so I laboriously slid on my butt/side/back down the scree toward the sun (it was still cool in the shade), while JWS retrieved the packs before joining me. At one point, a very helpful man, Walter Suttle from Salem, assisted us.

Around 2:00 p.m., after sliding down the scree for approximately several hundred feet, we did make contact with Deputy Greg Klein from the Linn County Sheriff's Office, who was incredibly professional and helpful. We talked about a plan to extract us. Around 3:30 p.m. and with help from the Corvallis SAR, a Blackhawk helicopter from the 1042nd National Army

Guard reeled me up in a basket. JWS was hauled up on the Jungle Penetrater. I was treated in the Salem emergency room for a fractured talus. At the time of this writing, I am recuperating well.

Analysis

1. Climb with someone in whom you have complete confidence. My wife was/is absolutely amazing.
2. Tell people where you are going and what you are doing.
3. While I have mixed feelings about the use of cell phones in a wilderness area, in this case it was extremely helpful. We'll never rely on a cell phone, but having one that works can make a big difference in how long it takes to get out and the severity of your injury.
4. A wilderness first aid class and training with the Obsidians helped us tremendously in terms of making a plan to help ourselves as much as possible.
5. Appreciate and thank your local SAR groups. Without them, extracting ourselves would have been very difficult.
6. The Salem hospital could not have been more professional or helpful. They were very impressive. (Source: The climber, who wishes to remain anonymous.)

FALL ON ROCK, INADEQUATE PROTECTION
Oregon, Mount Washington, West Face

On Thursday, July 29, Thomas Siefert (46) and Gary Gentz (50) were making their first attempt at climbing the West Face of Mount Washington in the Oregon Cascades. *Oregon High*, a 1991 climbing guide for the Oregon Cascades by Jeff Thomas, details several west side routes to the summit at 7,794 feet. The two men were reported overdue and a Search and Rescue action was initiated. The Jefferson County Sheriff's Camp Sherman Hasty Team reached the site on Saturday morning and confirmed their deaths from a mountain climbing accident.

Jefferson County Sheriff's Sargent Mark Foster conducted an investigation on the scene and filed a report of several pages with photographs of the site. The details of that report are included herein. Initial news stories of the accident referred to equipment failure perhaps mid-way up the face leading to local speculation about the quality of the rock on the West Face.

Evidence found at the scene indicates that the two men fell from near the top of the face, about 400 vertical feet. There was no gear on the rope, indicating it was not anchored to the rock at the time of the fall. One climber may have been working with his gear at the time he fell, based on an unlocked carabiner on his harness and loose gear—an older model belay plate and a runner with two carabiners, at an initial impact point. Based on the position of the rope at the scene, one man fell first and when the rope played out, he pulled the other climber off the cliff.

It is not known whether Mr. Siefert and Mr. Gentz were ascending or descending at the time of the accident. (Source: Robert Speik)

FALL ON ROCK, PROTECTION PULLED OUT, EXCEEDING ABILITIES
Oregon, Smith Rock State Park, Godzilla

Mark Kent (42) and his father, Terry Kent (64), arrived at Smith Rock State Park on a Saturday morning, September 18, to find that the trad climbs they had researched were taken by other climbers. They found Godzilla around the corner near Monkey Face, a 5.8 climb rated one star by Alan Watts in his *Climber's Guide to Smith Rock.*

Godzilla is a traditional unbolted climb given a mixed review by Watts for its climbing, including a dirty flair and a 5.8 under-cling at the top of the route. Godzilla requires gear to three inches according to Watts.

Terry Kent is a past Climb Leader with the Portland based Mazamas club. Terry belayed as Mark worked his way up the route. Near the top, Mark set a flexible shaft cam in a two-inch horizontal crack and climbed upward over a bulge. About four feet above his last piece and with clear air below the bulge, Mark found nowhere to go and, after warning his belayer, he dropped off.

Mark remembers a jerk as the last piece pulled out, before falling an estimated 25 feet to a ledge. He landed flat-footed on the ledge and then fell over backward, striking his head and hanging upside down. He was wearing a helmet that may have prevented him from losing consciousness.

Terry lowered his son toward the ground as Mark made his way through the complexity of the climb. They were alone in this part of the park. They called 911 from their cell phone. A Ranger appeared and soon two firemen charged with rescues at Smith. Mark was given morphine. The four carried Mark down the steep narrow trail to the Crooked River where other firemen were rigging a boat to a waiting ambulance. Mark was released from the hospital with his x-rays and soft casts. He returned to work five weeks later and is mountaineering again.

Analysis

Mark suggests that climbers create a redundant anchor below a crux move. He is concerned about the soft nature of the rock in this part of Smith which does not protect well. He feels, in retrospect, that this route was a bit beyond his current level.

FALL ON SNOW—DISLODGED ROCK, FAILURE TO TEST HOLDS, POOR POSITION, CLIMBING UNROPED AND ALONE
Oregon, Mount Hood, South Side

While ascending the Hogsback on Mount Hood's South Side route on September 30, Patrick Marcuson (63) dislodged rotten rock, causing him to slide about 200 feet, flying over the bergschrund. Despite losing his ice ax, he stopped sliding before reaching the fumarole. He dragged himself up to the safety of the Hogsback. He had fractured his leg. Unsuccessful in attracting attention, he lowered himself about 1,000 feet to a remnant structure where he splinted his leg using abandoned timbers. He survived the night under a tarp and made voice contact with two climbers the next morning, who notified authorities. Portland Mountain Rescue lowered him in a litter about 1,000 feet to a waiting snowcat.

Analysis

Late season climbs on exposed volcanic rock are predictably hazardous. Solo climbers must be particularly self-reliant on communicating their situation (signaling devices, radios, alert by family or friends when overdue, etc). It is worth noting that Marcuson was able to keep his crampons off the snow surface during his slide, thus preventing a tumbling fall. (Source: From a report by Jeff Sheetz, Portland Mountain Rescue)

FALL ON ICE, INADEQUATE PROTECTION
Oregon, Mount Hood, Sandy Glacier

On November 4, Kenny Dale Kasselder and Shaun Olcott (both 37) had crossed the Sandy Glacier, roped, and were beginning to ascend the headwall. One of them slipped and pulled the other off, as they had not placed any protection. They fell about 100 feet, landing in a crevasse. Olcott suffered a broken arm while Kasselder had injured his back. He lapsed into unconsciousness and died. Olcott was carrying a cell phone and was able to place a distress call to 911.

Analysis

They were simply low on the headwall when the accident occurred and had not yet placed any anchors, yet the fall was still sufficient to sustain significant injuries. After the rescue, Olcott reported that his helmet was shattered.

Readers will recall the most dramatic example of the risks of non-anchored rope travel on Mount Hood. On May 30, 2002, one climber slipped at the Pearly Gates on the South Side. He started a "domino" effect, sweeping the rest of his rope team and three other teams down the mountain. Nine total climbers landed into the bergschrund. Three climbers were killed, and four were seriously injured. (Steve Rollins, Portland Mountain Rescue)

(Editor's Note: On March 13, Beau Clark (30) died from a heart attack while climbing with friends on Broughton's Bluff. He had made it to a ledge. His friends said they heard a weird noise, and when they looked down., he was hanging about 30 feet above the ground. This is not considered to be a climbing accident, but worthy of mention.)

FALL ON ROCK—LOWERING ERROR, COMMUNICATION PROBLEM
Utah, Big Cottonwood Canyon

On June 16, Doug Grennan (18) and eight friends were top-roping sport climbs in the upper S-Curves area of Big Cottonwood Canyon. Doug was climbing a 5.10 route on the right side of the buttress, most likely Urban Sprawl (10a). When Doug reached the chains, he clipped in and cleaned the draws, as no one else planned to climb the route. He untied, threaded the rope through the chains, and tied back in. At this point he was still on belay, but with lots of slack in the rope. His plan was to have his belayer lower him. Because of an overhang below him, he and the belayer had a hard time seeing or hearing each other. Doug leaned out for a better look and yelled, "Take."

As he did, his feet slipped and he fell 60 feet to the ground, with the rope running through the belay device. He suffered a fractured sacrum, and bruised heels and sternum. Two friends ran to the road to call for a rescue. SAR team members immobilized Doug in a bean-bag vacuum splint and lowered him five pitches down and across scree fields to the trail. Once at the road, he was transported to the hospital by ground ambulance.

Analysis

Even with lots of slack in the rope, an attentive belayer should be able to catch a top-rope fall without any difficulty. The problem is that in this situation, where the climber re-rigs at the top of the route, the belayer may stop paying close attention, since a fall is not expected.

The belayer was using an ATC, which is a fairly low-friction belay device. Once the rope starts sliding quickly, there is almost no way to stop the moving rope.

Communication problems between climber and belayer produce an accident in our area every few years. Doug could have minimized the need for communication by rappelling down instead of being lowered. This is also a better choice for preserving the chains at the top of the route. (Tom Moyer, Salt Lake County Sheriff's Search and Rescue)

(Editor's Note: There was another Utah rappel/lowering incident reported in which the climber failed to tie his webbing sling properly. The knot came undone when weighted and he fell 30 feet to the ground, sustaining only bruises!)

VARIOUS FALLS ON ROCK, SOME SOLO, SOME INADEQUATELY PROTECTED, ETC.
Utah, Various Locations

We received some sketchy reports on several other accidents in Utah. They are summarized as follows.

On March 2, Robert Moor (35) fell 100 feet to his death when the ice he was attached to broke off. He was climbing with a friend in Sanpete County's Maple Canyon when the ice broke away from the face. Moore died on impact. It is suspected that weather related freeze/thaw was a contributing factor.

At 7:00 p.m. on May 29, a 21-year-old man was free-soloing with some friends at the Moss Ledges picnic area when he apparently slipped on a wet rock and fell backward into the creek. Witnesses said the man fell approximately 15 feet and landed on his head. County search and rescue volunteers and paramedics reached the man quickly and a life-flight helicopter was on hand waiting to transport, but the victim died at the scene.

On July 11, Tim Roberts (36) of Salt Lake City, sustained several broken vertebrae when he fell 20 feet after his climbing rope slipped (NB: Assume belay slipped) and his partner was unable to regain control. Dispatchers from the Utah County Sheriff's office received a call reporting the accident at 9:00 a.m. Lone Peak Fire District Paramedics treated Roberts at the scene. The canyon was closed for several hours in order to bring in a helicopter to airlift him to L.D.S. Hospital in Salt Lake City. Police report that Roberts and his partner were both experienced climbers and were using appropriate equipment.

On July 14, a 25-year-old man was climbing next to a waterfall in Coal Pit Gulch in Little Cottonwood Canyon when one of the rocks he was using as a handhold pulled out. The man was free-soloing and fell into a very steep and treacherous area. He suffered facial lacerations and a possible broken ankle and was unable to move. The man's friend ran down the trail to get help and encountered a third person with a cell phone who notified rescue personnel. Several hours of highly technical rescue work were required to bring the victim out of the gulch.

On July 18, Patrick Desisto (19) was rescued after being stranded on a ledge for 19 hours near Bridal Veil Falls in Provo Canyon. A large boulder had fallen on his hands. Desisto suffered lacerations and broken bones in several fingers.

On August 11, a 50-year-old man was rappelling into Pine Creek Canyon from the north rim when he found that his rope did not reach to the canyon floor. When he attempted to stop his downward movement, he turned upside down and rappelled off the end of his rope, falling 15 feet to the canyon floor. EMS personnel and rescuers attended to him and raised him 100 feet to the rim. He sustained fractures to four ribs and his left femur.

On December 17, a highly experienced rock climber was killed after apparently falling 400 feet from a peak in Ogden Canyon. The body of Kenneth Gigi of Syracuse was recovered on the afternoon of the 18th following an extensive search and recovery effort. Gigi went climbing near Malan's Peak in Ogden on the December 17. He was due back at his home by 5:00 p.m. but never made it. About 9:00 p.m. his family called the Sheriff's office to report him missing. Search crews found two of Gigi's friends who were also looking for him, and they pointed searchers to the area Gigi frequented. At 11:00 p.m. a group consisting of Sheriff's searchers and friends spotted Gigi's body in a chute below the face of the peak. It appeared that he had slipped while climbing and had fallen or slid approximately 400 feet. Gigi was solo climbing with no gear or helmet, only a backpack. The best theory is that for whatever reason, he began climbing and was soon in a position where the safest escape was to try to climb out of the canyon, followed by a slip on ice or snow.

Analysis

Not much can be said with so few details. The ones with obvious errors need no comment. An interesting conclusion to the man who rappelled off the end of his rope is that the leader of his five-person team was issued a citation for not having a canyoneering permit. Of greater concern should have been why no knot was tied in the end of the rope. (Source: Jed Williamson)

FALL ON ROCK—NOT ANCHORED AT TOP OF CLIFF, INEXPERIENCE
Utah, Big Cottonwood Canyon, Storm Mountain Amphitheater

On October 10, Amberly Rogers (20) fell at the Storm Mountain Amphitheater while attempting to set up a top-rope. She was on a buttress just west of the climb Big in Japan (12b). The area she was in is accessed by a short scramble from the west and has no established climbing routes on it. She was planning to set a top-rope on the buttress and was either about to throw the rope or was in the process of throwing the rope down to her climbing partners when she slipped. It is not known whether she had set her anchor yet, but if she had, then she did not clip in to it. No gear was left at the spot. She took about a 25-foot high-angle slide/tumble, followed by a 25-foot free-fall to the ground.

The area in which she fell is in the Storm Mountain Picnic Area. Paramedics from Salt Lake County Fire were able to reach her easily, and transported her by Air-med helicopter to the hospital. Amberly died from her injuries several days later.

Analysis

In an exposed spot, it's clearly better to rig a good anchor first and tie in to it before doing anything like throwing the rope where you might risk a fall. At the time of the accident, Amberly had been climbing only about a month. (Tom Moyer, Salt Lake County Sheriff's Search and Rescue)

(Editor's Note: Tom Moyer submitted a few other reports, involving a stranded climber who had thrown his rope down, loss of control on glissade, and a protection failure following a fall.)

RAPPEL FAILURE—MULTIPLE CAUSES
Washington, Frenchman's Coulee

Around 2:00 p.m. on March 7, Robert Peruchini (41) and his partner, Ms. Teri Martin (52), climbed the traditional basalt pillar route known as "Pumping the Pigeon" (5.8) on Sunshine Wall at Frenchman's Coulee, five miles east of Vantage. Peruchini led the climb; Martin seconded and cleaned the gear. They topped out and prepared a rappel from the chains on a pillar-top adjacent to the route. After passing the 10.5-mm, 220-foot-long Edelweiss rope through the fixed anchor chains, both climbers tossed a coil of rope over the side. Peruchini's strand was on the west side of the rap station and Martin's coil was tossed to the east side of the anchors. Peruchini tossed his coil first with Martin tossing her coil seconds later. The east (left) strand of rope fell or was blown by the wind into a notch between the anchor pillar and the adjacent pillar and was thus obstructed from full view.

Peruchini then sat down facing outward with his legs straddling the anchor chains and prepared the rope for his rappel. Martin asked him, "Is it down?" Peruchini answered affirmatively. Peruchini may have seen the west strand of rope (to his right) piled up on the ground and mistook it for both strands and proceeded to rappel on the doubled rope. Unbeknownst to Peruchini, one side of the rope was lengthened, possibly due to the wind catching it, and the other side was shortened to about 12 feet. Peruchini rappelled on both strands for approximately 12 feet and then down off the short strand of the rope but grabbed it after it passed through his Black Diamond Standard ATC belay/rappel device.

Peruchini hung with both hands onto both ends for 30-40 seconds before calling to his partner, "Teri, help me! I've rapped off the end of my rope!" Martin, who was standing ten feet back from the cliff's edge sorting gear, ran up, clipped herself into the anchors with a runner and peered over the edge of the pillar. She saw Peruchini hanging approximately 12 feet below her and told him to try to place his feet on a pillar top that she estimated to be six to 12 inches below his feet. He struggled for approximately 15 seconds and then lost his grip and fell 58 feet before striking a pillar top.

Witnesses reported seeing Peruchini strike the lower pillar feet first. He then cart-wheeled leftward another 20 feet down the boulders to the trail, breaking and losing his Black Diamond Half Dome helmet in the tumble and impacts. Peruchini then bounced and rolled off the narrow trail and dropped another 40 feet off the Lower Sunshine Wall (a.k.a. The Henhouse Wall) and slid 20 feet down the talus slope where he came to a stop.

Citizen first-aiders from the Spokane Mountaineers Club performed CPR for 45 minutes while awaiting paramedics to arrive on scene. Citizen first-aiders and a nurse performed all initial care. Care was handed over to Grant County Fire Department EMTs. Airlift operations were directed by two Tacoma Mountain Rescuers (TMRU) who were climbing nearby. They back-boarded Peruchini and rigged a lower system. They lowered him 100 feet and assisted loading him in the Army MAST basket litter. Patient care was given over to the MAST medic. Peruchini was transported by MAST a quarter mile to the parking lot where Grant County paramedics pronounced him dead and transported him by ambulance to the Grant County Coroner in Moses Lake.

Analysis

On Sunday, March 14, rescue personnel from Central Washington Mountain Rescue performed an investigation and reenactment of the rappel.

Several small but important factors contributed to this accident. Through interviews with the primary witness, Ms. Martin, secondary witnesses, climbing partners, and empirical observations, it was determined the following factors played a role in this accident.

- Communication was poor between the climbers due to the wind-noise and proximity to one another.
- The easterly wind may have moved the rope into the notch between pillars on the east thus hiding the end from view.
- Peruchini was only able to see the west strand of rope safely on the ground. If the east strand of rope was in the notch it was invisible to him beyond eight feet.
- The wind may have caused the rope to travel through the anchor chains resulting in one strand becoming substantially shorter than the other.
- Peruchini had rock climbed three days in a row after a long layoff and was nursing a rotator cuff injury to his right shoulder. Fatigue may have played a part in his decision-making ability and observation acuity.
- Fatigue and shoulder pain may have reduced his physical ability to hang by his hands from the ropes and/or regain a safe hold on the pillar.

(Source: Edited from a very thorough report primarily authored by Andrew P. Jenkins, PhD, WEMT, of the Central Washington Mountain Rescue Investigative Team)

SLIP/FALL ON SNOW AND ROCK
Washington, Mount Rainier, Liberty Ridge

Climber Scott Richards (42) called Mount Rainier National Park on a cell phone requesting a rescue for his climbing partner Peter Cooley (39) at 6:10 a.m. on May 15. The two-person team was ascending Liberty Ridge near 12,000 feet when Cooley's crampon caught and he fell while leading. Richards was on the opposite side of the ridge-crest when the accident occurred and was able to stop the fall using a hip belay. Cooley had fallen approximately 30 feet and hit his head, sustaining severe head trauma including a skull fracture as well as injuries to his left arm and leg. At roughly 6:30 a.m., Ranger Mike Gauthier advised Richards via cell phone to chop out a platform, secure their tent, and stabilize and prepare Cooley for a lengthy evacuation. Scheduled cell phone calls were arranged to conserve the team's cell phone batteries.

An Oregon Army National Guard Chinook and contract helicopter and climbing field teams were assembled for the rescue. At that time the weather was deteriorating rapidly, and forecasts predicted large amounts of precipitation. On its initial reconnaissance, the contract helicopter approached Liberty Ridge, but due to whiteout conditions was forced to land on the Carbon Glacier at 8,000 feet and wait for a clearing. Because of the increasing clouds near the mountain, the Oregon National Guard Chinook helicopter was sent to Rimrock, WA, instead of Kautz Heli-base inside the park to connect with an aviation rescue team of NPS rangers and Rainier Mountaineering guides (RMI).

An air-assisted rescue seemed uncertain because of weather conditions, so a field team of two climbing rangers was hastily assembled and dispatched to make a quick ascent of Liberty Ridge. The advanced climbing rescue team of David Gottlieb and Chris Olson departed Ipsut Creek Campground Saturday at 4:00 p.m. Heavy rain and snowfall slowed Gottlieb and Olson, forcing them to bivouac on lower Curtis Ridge that evening. A second team consisting of five climbing rangers also assembled at Ipsut Creek Campground. They carried extra supplies and prepared to support the advance team for a lengthy ground evacuation.

Late afternoon clearing around the mountain allowed the contract helicopter to depart the Carbon Glacier and return to Kautz Heli-base. Richards was apprised of the rescue efforts and difficulties. He prepared for a night on the mountain at the accident site with Cooley.

Via cell phone the next morning, Richards reported that Cooley was in and out of consciousness all night and was unable to eat or drink. The weather remained inclement for much of the day.

A team of five climbers from Tacoma Mountain Rescue (TMR) departed Ipsut Creek Campground at 11:00 a.m. after a briefing at Longmire. Another TMR team of two staffed the Camp Muir hut. In all, over 60 people joined in the rescue effort; the event generated international media attention.

At noon, the Chinook team attempted a flight with rescue personnel but heavy cloud cover and foul weather caused the mission to be aborted. Difficult climbing conditions and harsh weather made progress for the ground/climbing teams very arduous. Rangers Gottlieb and Olson worked through whiteout conditions and deep snow on the Carbon Glacier to prepare a field operations basecamp at 8,800 feet in the Carbon Glacier basin below Willis Wall. A six-person climbing ranger team later joined them while the TMR team prepared a camp at 7,200 feet on lower Curtis Ridge. At 6:35 p.m. the weather briefly cleared above the Carbon Glacier, allowing the contract helicopter to conduct reconnaissance at the accident site and deliver a sling load of supplies, including a radio to replace Richard's dead cell phone.

On the evening of May 16, climbing rangers Gottlieb and Charlie Borgh prepared for an ascent of Liberty Ridge on the morning of the 17th. They planned to access the accident site, a 50-55 degree ice slope at roughly 12,000 feet, evaluate the scene and determine the feasibility for a helicopter evacuation or, if impossible, a technical rope rescue. Behind them climbing rangers Johnson, Olson, Anderson, Sherred, and Loewen, laden with camping and rigging equipment, climbed to Thumb Rock, and established an advanced camp. Ranger Glenn Kessler remained at basecamp to manage field operations.

On May 17, the contract helicopter attempted to sling-load additional supplies to the climbing teams. However, the weather again thwarted the aviation operation. The Chinook insertion team also attempted a mountain flight but was unable due to weather and was forced to return to Yakima. Additional supplies and equipment were ferried via ground teams from Ipsut Creek campground to 7,200 feet on Lower Curtis Ridge.

Around noon, Gottlieb and Borgh arrived at the 11,800 foot accident site. Gottlieb attempted a medical assessment and relayed information to medical control via cell phone. Only limited care could be provided due to the conditions and patient and rescuer safety concerns. The team also prepared the area and set ice anchors preparing for a technical rescue. The weather improved throughout the afternoon and at 2:30 p.m., the contract helicopter delivered a sling load to the 8,800 foot camp, while a supply cache was transported to Thumb Rock. The stabilizing weather also allowed the Chinook insertion team to head for the mountain at 4:30 p.m.

As the Chinook lumbered over the mountain at 5:03 p.m., Cooley was extracted via vertical litter hoist. He was immediately flown to Madigan Hospital and, very sadly, pronounced dead. Gottlieb and Borgh descended Liberty Ridge with Richards to spend the night at Thumb Rock.

Analysis

Cooley and Richards were accomplished climbers. This accident was not a result of any lapse in judgment or lack of skill. Cooley's short, but ultimately fatal fall seems to be the result of an unfortunate misstep. Cooley was wearing a climbing helmet, but sometime during the fall, he hit his head on a rock that contacted his temple just under the helmet brim. That impact eventually caused his death.

Any serious injury on a remote route at high elevation can be life-threatening due to the difficulty of access and evacuation. This accident highlights the difficulties of high altitude rescue on technical terrain, particularly when exacerbated by poor weather. Aviation is a key element of many successful upper-mountain rescues of climbers with serious injuries. When weather precludes flying, the survival of a critically injured climber is often compromised.

The fact that Richards was able to care for his climbing partner for almost 60 hours on a small exposed platform that he chopped in ice during poor weather speaks highly of him as an alpinist, rescuer, and friend. The NPS strongly recommends choosing climbing partners carefully, considering not only the ability to reach the summit, but how a partner will perform in the event of an emergency or stressful situation.

While many were saddened by the outcome of this extended event after so much effort by so many people, it should be noted that the rescue was also a great success in that Richards returned safely and no rescuers were hurt. Without his climbing partner, Richards would have been placed in the difficult position of soloing the route in order to reach safety. (Source: Mike Gauthier, SAR Ranger, Mount Rainier National Park)

(Editor's Note: Another fatality and serious injury occurred on Liberty Ridge on June 3, when two climbers fell several hundred feet from just below the Black Pyramid.)

LOSS OF CONTROL—VOLUNTARY GLISSADE, FAULTY USE OF CRAMPONS, INADEQUATE PROTECTION
Washington, Mount Rainier, Emmons/Winthrop Glacier Route

On June 3, Doug Thiel (40) and his two climbing partners summited Mount Rainier via the Emmons Glacier Route. On their descent, Thiel started to experience a great deal of knee pain. The pain became so intense that he preferred to glissade instead of walking down. Thiel decided to glissade while roped and wearing crampons. It was the team's intent to descend in this fashion back to Camp Schurman.

At 11,600 feet, Thiel hit an icy section and was unable to stop his slide. He slid uncontrollably past his partners and pulled them off their feet. All three fell 75-100 feet before Thiel's two partners arrested. Thiel sustained a lower left leg injury in the process and recalled the rope wrapping around his leg, which he feels contributed to the injury.

At 3:30 p.m., the Park received a cell phone call from Thiel's team detailing the accident and requesting assistance. With a large rescue and body recovery already in progress on Liberty Ridge, the I.C. dispatched a reserve climbing ranger team to the site of the new accident. Climbing rangers Stefan Lofgren and Stoney Richards were inserted on the Emmons Glacier via light helicopter near 11,300 feet. They ascended to the accident site, assessed Thiel and then carried him to a Landing Zone and from there he was flown to the Kautz Heli-base where he was transferred to an ambulance.

Analysis

Thiel wanted to avoid requesting outside help while descending. Unfortunately, glissading, particularly on the upper mountain glaciers while wearing crampons, is dangerous. It would have been safer and more efficient for Thiel's partners to have steadily lowered him in a sitting position, one rope-length at a time. On most sections they could have simply lowered him hand over hand. On steeper sections, they could have lowered him off set protection (pickets, ice axes, etc). In the end, it is always best to avoid glissading. Glissading with crampons is never a good idea. (Source: Mike Gauthier, SAR Ranger, Mount Rainier National Park)

AVALANCHE
Washington, Mount Rainier, Liberty Ridge

Luke Casady and Ansel Vizcaya (both 29) departed White River Campground on Friday June 11 for a planned ascent of Liberty Ridge. The exact details of the subsequent 48 hours may never be known, but the facts uncovered during the subsequent search, body recoveries, and ensuing investigation suggest the following:

Casady and Vizcaya, experienced climbers, camped along Curtis Ridge on Friday and began the ascent up Liberty Ridge early Saturday morning. It is likely the pair climbed past Thumb Rock, around and continued up the ridge as the first signs of incoming weather appeared. With the winds building and the visibility decreasing the climbers continued pushing forward. By early evening, the reports at Camp Muir included significantly higher winds and heavy snowfall. Casady and Vizcaya were somewhere high on Liberty Ridge, and probably realized that they would have to hunker down and wait out the storm.

Through the night, winds hammered the mountain, blowing snow from some areas while building large slabs in others. This was an uncomfortable night for climbers everywhere on Mount Rainier. Heavy snowfall and high winds destroyed several tents at Camp Muir.

By Sunday morning several inches of snow had fallen, but more importantly, the high winds had deposited large amounts of snow on leeward slopes. Casady and Vizcaya were probably camped between 12,900 feet and 13,500 feet above the Black Pyramid. Sometime during that night or the next day, Casady and Vizcaya were caught in a large avalanche. The avalanche probably released several hundred feet above them but below Liberty Cap. The avalanche most likely encompassed them and the entire upper route; everything was pushed down the 4,000 foot Liberty Wall to the Carbon Glacier. Neither climber could have survived the fall.

It took many reconnaissance flights over several days to locate the bodies.

Analysis

Casady and Vizcaya were found in their climbing harnesses but unroped. The rope found had no knots in it. Their packs were largely packed, yet the pair had their parkas on. It appeared as though they were either still in camp, in the process of setting up or in the process of breaking camp when the avalanche occurred.

The fracture line noted on Liberty Wall was direct evidence of a large slab avalanche whose crown extended halfway to Ptarmigan Ridge, some 250 meters. The crown was only observed from the air, but appeared to vary in thickness from about 25-100cm. Whether or not this crown belonged to the avalanche that swept the climbers to their deaths is uncertain, as a smaller slide could have caught them. Large avalanches were occurring on the mountain following the Saturday night storm.

Other observations during the search indicated that large avalanches had run on other slopes in the general vicinity of Liberty and Ptarmigan Ridges. There had been no climbers on these slopes so it was concluded that most slides were naturally triggered events. It seems unlikely that there were any climbers above Casady and Vizcaya, yet this remains unknown. The climbers had indicated when they registered that they had avalanche transceivers with them though neither was wearing one. A transceiver, however, would have provided no protection from such an avalanche.

It is important to note that snowstorms and avalanches do occur on Mount Rainier in the summer. Climbers during all seasons should be prepared to assess avalanche issues. (Source: Mike Gauthier, SAR Ranger, Mount Rainier National Park)

STRANDED, EXCEEDING ABILITIES, INCOMPATIBLE PARTNERS—POOR COMMUNICATION
Washington, Mount Rainier, Liberty Ridge

Bruce Penn (43) and Al Hancock (44) departed White River to climb Liberty Ridge on June 13. It took them three days to reach the base. On the third day, while looking at Liberty Ridge, Penn voiced concern to Hancock about the steepness of the route and his ability to climb it.

They spent the day talking about descent, but decided to reevaluate their plan at the base of Liberty Ridge. On the fourth day, June 16, an apprehensive Penn decided to start up the ridge with Hancock setting anchors and belaying every pitch. It took 14 hours for the pair to reach Thumb Rock. Both individuals were exhausted and dehydrated when they finally arrived.

Penn knew that it should only take four to six hours to reach Thumb Rock from lower Curtis Ridge. He was surprised that other climbing parties were not placing protection and climbing the lower ridge without belay. He then realized that their climbing method was not practical for the route.

On the fifth morning, Penn knew that he could not complete the climb and called 911 on his cell phone to ask for assistance. He did not discuss this with Hancock and only informed him after the call had already occurred. That call reached Supervisory Climbing Ranger Mike Gauthier. During the conversation, Penn stated that his team could not go up or down but added that there were no injuries and they had enough food and fuel for a few days. Since there was no obvious urgency and because an active SAR was already in progress on Liberty Ridge, Gauthier informed Penn that they would have to wait for a rescue or assistance.

At 12:44 p.m., Penn called again stating that he "...could not climb up or down from Thumb Rock." Penn again acknowledged that he and his partner were okay, but that their arms were quite sore, they were dehydrated and that they had bad vibes about the route. Hancock felt that their best option was to continue the climb up and over, but refused to go back down. Penn was unwilling to continue up or down even with additional supplies and gear the NPS offered to drop at their location. It was explained to Penn that another more urgent SAR was in progress and that they would need to remain where they were until more personnel and resources were available.

At 7:30 p.m. Penn again called the Park requesting a helicopter rescue. When told that their rescue would still require a belayed down-climb, Penn seemed unwilling to cooperate. He said, "I just want to be off the mountain."

On the sixth day, arrangements were made with the Oregon National Guard for a helicopter hoist of the pair as rescue and recovery efforts remained ongoing for Casady and Vizcaya. Rangers made two airdrops—food, fuel, and a cell phone—for Penn and Hancock at Thumb Rock.

On the seventh day, an Oregon National Guard Chinook helicopter flew to the scene with three climbing rangers aboard. Ranger David Gottlieb was lowered to Thumb Rock via hoist and assisted both climbers back into the helicopter. The climbers were successfully removed from the mountain that day.

Analysis

Penn and Hancock met on a guided climb of Mount McKinley the previous year. They had not climbed together before, but did discuss and research Mount Rainier and Liberty Ridge extensively. Some climbers often overlook the important aspect of climbing relationships and partner compatibility. The importance of a skills assessment, common goals and similar abilities are sometimes overshadowed by the excitement of summiting the mountain or doing a route.

A commendable aspect of this incident was that the team realized things were not going well and pulled back before getting injured. The NPS recognizes that people commit errors in judgment and make mistakes, but suggests that climbers not proceed when originally presented with questionable situations.

As a reminder, Liberty Ridge requires a substantial amount of physical strength, technical skill, effective communication and comfort with a heavy pack on steep ice for 6,000 feet of climbing. (Source: Mike Gauthier, SAR Ranger, Mount Rainier National Park)

FALL ON ICE, INADEQUATE PROTECTION, INADEQUATE BELAY
Washington, Mount Baker, North Ridge

Elain Fu (33) and I (Stephen Ramsey, 33) were simul-climbing up the ice cliff on the North Ridge of Mount Baker. I was in the lead. At 6:30 a.m., I reached a slightly overhanging lip of ice, about five feet in height. The elevation was about 9,700 feet, and the angle of the face below the lip was about 70 degrees. I placed a screw and traversed to the left about 20 feet, looking for a spot to climb over the lip. I stopped at a point where the lip had a crack in it, and inched up towards the lip on my front-points. During this time, Elain gained some ground on me, and we believe that some slack was generated in our rope system. Without stopping to place a screw or set a belay, I reached up and tried to test to see if I could reach the top of the lip with my ice tool.

At that time, a front-point skittered out of the ice and I fell backwards. I fell about 40 feet, penduluming to the climber's right, sliding down the ice face on my side. After much acceleration, I caught a crampon on an ice bulge, severely breaking my lower leg multiple fracture: tib/fib).

Analysis

I made a series of mistakes in rapid succession. I was feeling anxious about finding the best way to pass the ice lip, but instead of making me more careful, this anxiousness led me to rush and make mistakes. I neglected to place a screw immediately after executing the 20-foot traverse to protect myself from a pendulum fall. After seeing that the lip was slightly overhanging, I should have set up a belay before attempting to climb over the lip. Better communication with the second would have also helped to prevent the accident, because Elain would have cautioned me against attempting the lip without a solid belay from two screws.

My wife Elain, Bellingham Mountain Rescue, Naval Air Station Whidbey SAR, and Whatcom County SAR did a fantastic job of rescuing me from the mountain. Their timeliness and professionalism enabled me to be rescued the night of the accident, which directly improved my chances for recovering full joint function. (Source: Stephen Ramsey, who also wrote a long narrative account that he made available for several months on the web)

SLIP ON ICE–DISLOCATED SHOULDER
Washington, Mount Rainier, Kautz Glacier

On June 30, Dallas Baker (27) sustained a dislocated shoulder while descending the upper ice pitch of the Kautz Glacier near 11,800 feet. He was facing the glacier slope with his ice tools in the ice when his footing gave way. He was able to use one ax and catch the fall, but strained and dislocated his shoulder during the slip. Unable to reset the shoulder, his partner Alex Carroll called 911 seeking help from the NPS. The two slowly continued their descent to Camp Hazard.

A Hughes 500D helicopter was diverted from ongoing aviation operation to assist with the incident. Climbing ranger Stoney Richards was inserted at a small LZ on the cleaver separating the Turtle Snowfield from the Kautz Glacier around 11,000 feet. Richards climbed to the team and assessed Baker. By this time Baker's shoulder had reduced on its own. Despite

Baker's improved condition, he was assisted back to the LZ and extracted with Richards to Kautz Heli-base.

Analysis

Baker was able to prevent a substantial fall by holding onto his planted ice tool. His dislocated shoulder seems to have been a much better option than falling down the 45-degree ice slope. The team was using a running belay as they down-climbed the route, so hopefully if he had fallen he would have been caught as soon as the rope between the climbers came under tension.

The result of a fall of this type, even if the running belay protection held, would probably have caused more serious injuries than a dislocated shoulder. A very similar accident at approximately the same location occurred six weeks later. In the second accident, however, a longer fall resulted and the running protection (two ice screws) ripped out. (Source: Mike Gauthier, SAR Ranger, Mount Rainier National Park)

LOSS OF CONTROL—VOLUNTARY GLISSADE
Washington, Mount Rainier National Park, Unicorn Peak

On the morning of July 24, a four-person team from the Mazamas Climbing Club set out to climb Unicorn Peak in the Tatoosh Range. On the descent from the summit at roughly 2:30 p.m., Joska Rettig (50) lost control while glissading a steep snowfield. She sustained a serious injury to her left knee and leg when she impacted the rocks at the base of the snowfield. One member of the team was sent to seek assistance from the NPS while climb leader Jae Ellers splinted Rettig's leg with an ice ax and started her crawling back towards the road. Her progress was exceedingly slow, but very admirable.

Ellers was beginning a belay of Rettig down the steep loose rock gully feeding Snow Lake when climbing rangers Glenn Kessler and Thomas Payne arrived. The rangers assisted in Rettig's descent until they met another NPS team of rescuers. That team placed Rettig on a backboard and then into a litter for what became a night carry-out to the trailhead. Upon reaching the Snow Lake trailhead, Rettig was transferred to an awaiting ambulance.

Analysis

Don't glissade. It is safer to walk than to glissade. Glissading is a tempting option that often results in lost equipment and injuries. The slope on which Rettig lost control was a combination of hard and soft snow. It is very likely that Rettig was able to control her speed on the upper sections of the slope where the sun had been shining for hours, but was unable to slow herself on the lower, mostly shaded section. (Source: Mike Gauthier, SAR Ranger, Mount Rainier National Park)

(Editor's Note: Ranger Gauthier's experience with those who glissade in the park has been mostly negative. Back in the days of long ice axes, we used to teach standing glissades. With the third point of contact and in an almost skiing position, there is

more control than if just on two boots with a short ax in hand in case you fall. Sitting glissades with one's ax pick as the controlling brake at one's side is safer than a standing glissade. Those of us who are experienced skiers and who know we will have an opportunity to glissade will continue to use that option. But if you are a neophyte, take Gauthier's advice.)

FALL ON GLACIER ICE, INADEQUATE PROTECTION, PROTECTION PULLED OUT
Washington, Mount Rainier, Kautz Glacier Route

On August 8 at 9:15 a.m., while leading the second icy pitch of the Kautz Glacier Route, Bryan Fry (28) fell on the 45-degree icy pitch. What protection had been placed between him and his partner, John Dufay (25), pulled out as Fry fell. Fry's fall jerked Dufay off the slope and the pair tumbled an estimated 400 to 600 feet before coming to rest in a shallow crevasse.

Dufay suffered multiple lacerations and contusions during the fall; Fry sustained several minor injuries and a badly broken ankle. Dufay assisted Fry onto a narrow shelf in the crevasse and made him as comfortable as possible before seeking help. Dufay unroped and descended the route and through the ice chute back towards Camp Hazard. In the ice chute above Camp Hazard, Dufay met an RMI guide, Lyndon Mallory, who radioed the NPS for help.

Due to the terrain at the accident site and the anticipated hazards involved in a carry-out, an air evacuation was the fastest and safest option available. At 11:20 a.m., ranger Glenn Kessler spoke directly with Dufay via radio and received a first-hand account of the situation. Mallory then ascend with Dufay back to the accident site and helped care for Fry. A helicopter hoist operation was arranged to evacuate Fry from the location.

At 4:52 p.m., an Oregon Army National Guard Blackhawk lifted off from Kautz Heli-base and flew to the accident site with ranger Kessler. Kessler was hoisted onto the glacier where Fry and Mallory were waiting. Fry was assessed, prepared for evacuation and hoisted back into the Blackhawk with Kessler. Mallory and Dufay descended on foot but were slowed by Dufay's injuries and exhaustion. The two bivvied around 9,000 feet and arrived at the Comet Falls Trailhead at noon the next day.

Analysis

Fry and Dufay were lucky not to have fallen farther, as the Kautz Glacier becomes an ice cliff only a few hundred feet below where they came to rest. Fry reported that he had only one or two 9cm ice screws placed when he fell.

Dufay recalls getting in position to arrest Fry's fall, but was unsuccessful stopping the fall due to the steep angle and icy conditions. He recalls slowing several times thinking the fall was over, only to be yanked downhill again. When he came to rest, he was balled up in the rope. Given the distance of their fall, it is impressive that both did not suffer more severe injuries.

While the Kautz Glacier route can be an ice-free snow climb until midseason, several parties have underestimated the difficulty of late season conditions. As the winter snow cover disappears and more ice presents itself, there is a need for more ice climbing equipment. It is difficult to predict how much ice climbing gear may be needed given the variety of conditions possible. It is best to prepare for the worst and bring a few extra screws. (Source: Mike Gauthier, SAR Ranger, Mount Rainier National Park)

LOSS OF CONTROL—VOLUNTARY GLISSADE, FAULTY USE OF CRAMPONS
Washington, Mount Rainier, Muir Snowfield

On October 3, shortly after 4:30 p.m., Chris Beoffoli (34) began his descent from Camp Muir. While descending near 7,800 feet on the Muir Snowfield, Beoffoli, according to a report from him, "...fell back and because it was steep, I started to pick up some speed. I didn't have my ice ax within reach and, even though I should have known better, I instinctively put my heel down to stop myself and the metal teeth (of his crampons) stuck into the snow while my body kept moving." This resulted in a severely fractured ankle

At 5:15 p.m. Mt. Rainier National Park received the 911 cell phone call requesting a rescue. Shortly after sunset, an eight person NPS ground evacuation team began their ascent to the accident site. They arrived on scene two hours later and assessed Beoffoli's condition, packaged and lowered him back to Paradise in a litter. They arrived at the trailhead at 1:00 a.m. Beoffoli was released into the care of his partner who drove him a hospital for treatment. (Source: Mike Gauthier, SAR Ranger, Mount Rainier National Park and a report from Mr. Beoffoli.)

AVALANCHE
Washington, Mount Rainier, Ingraham Glacier

On October 24, climbers Aaron Koester and Matt Little contemplated a summit ascent from their high camp at Cadaver Gap, but due to a late start the pair instead decided to train and explore and the crevasses on the Ingraham Glacier. Near 11,700 feet, the team entered a large cavernous crevasse close to the Disappointment Cleaver. They traversed some 75 yards into the crevasse and found an exit ramp out the other side. While ascending the 35-40 degree exit ramp, the snow slope fractured and slid.

The slab was estimated to be about eight to 14 inches thick and ran roughly 150 feet. The avalanche swept both climbers back into the crevasse. Koester was pinned against the ice wall of the crevasse and was completely buried by the debris. Little was partially buried; only his arm and head were exposed. Little spent about 30 minutes extricating himself from the entrapment before beginning the search for his partner. By the time he located and freed Koester's head, Koester had no pulse and was very blue.

Little left the accident site and descended the Ingraham Glacier back to high camp, packed up the team's equipment and continued down to Camp Muir. Along the descent, Little attempted to contact the authorities using a family service radio. A hunter picked up the transmission and notified the NPS of the accident at 4:58 p.m. Twenty minutes later, Little arrived at Camp Muir and called the Park on the Camp Muir emergency radio. After providing more specific information about the accident, Little descended to Paradise and met with park rangers.

The following day, climbing rangers Mike Gauthier, Bree Loewen, and Adrienne Sherred, with the assistance of an MD 500 contract helicopter, were inserted at Ingraham Flats, 11,000 feet. They climbed to the cavernous crevasse and performed the body recovery. An analysis of the fracture, slide, and ramp area was not possible however, due to lingering instability in the snowpack, time limitations and deteriorating weather. Koester's body was successfully recovered that day.

Analysis

A recent storm had deposited only a few inches of snow, but high winds preceding the climb had transported this snow significantly. Many areas were scoured; others had deep pockets of snow. Autumn is an atypical time for avalanche accidents; at that time of year the dangers of falling on hard ice, snow bridges collapsing, rockfall and icefall are generally more pressing. As this accident illustrates, climbers must evaluate the avalanche risks at any time of year.

The fact that these climbers chose to wear avalanche beacons on the day of the incident indicates an increased level of avalanche awareness. They knew that they were in avalanche terrain and that there was a possibility of a slide occurring. However, no assessments of the snow stability took place. It is possible that if the climbers had done an assessment, they may have recognized the snow instability and avoided the terrain trap.

As the use of avalanche transceivers has become more standard in alpine climbing, it's important for climbers to connect the reasoning of wearing such a device with the conditions. Donning a transceiver does not prevent the consequences of an avalanche. It's important not to let down your guard when wearing a transceiver. A false sense of safety lowers the level of situational awareness, causing many to ignore or misinterpret valuable information and signs. (Source: Mike Gauthier, SAR Ranger, Mount Rainier National Park)

FALL ON SNOW—UNABLE TO SELF-ARREST
Wyoming, Grand Teton National Park, Grand Teton

I met ranger Chris Harder at approximately 0830 hours at his residence at Beaver Creek on the morning of March 12. We had planned to go on a backcountry ski patrol up to the top of the peak 9,925 located immediately west of the Beaver Creek residential area. While at Beaver Creek I received a phone call from John Kidde at 0845, who reported that his friends, Matthew

Neuner (25) and Elizabeth Dyer (27), were overdue from their proposed one-day, winter ascent of the Grand Teton. Based on the information that he gave us, we decided to switch our proposed patrol area to Garnet Canyon. We left the Taggart Lake trailhead and made our way up and over the moraine to Bradley Lake and then proceeded up into Garnet Canyon. Just below the Platforms we met Hans Johnstone, an Exum mountain guide, who reported that while he was at the Lower Saddle he had heard cries for help up toward the Grand Teton. He had responded with a sleeping bag and a pad to the area of the Black Dike, contacted Neuner and Dyer, stabilized her, and then proceeded down the canyon to report the accident.

Johnstone reported that Dyer had fallen several hundred feet that morning while descending from an ascent of the Grand and had suffered a significant head injury with an associated loss of consciousness. She was stable when he left her, in a sleeping bag and on a pad, and attended by her climbing partner. Johnstone was accompanied by Mark Newcomb and Greg Seitz and I requested all of their assistance for the subsequent rescue operation. I also notified South District ranger Andy Fisher of the situation since he was to be the Incident Commander during this SAR. After our rendezvous, the five of us then skied down to the west shore of Bradley Lake to prepare a heli-spot for a pickup and shuttle to the Lower Saddle.

About 1700, Dyer was evacuated from the scene of the incident via short-haul and was flown down to a heli-spot near Park headquarters at Moose. Ranger Chris Harder attended the patient during the flight to the valley floor. The patient was transferred to air ambulance and taken to Eastern Idaho Regional Medical Center in Idaho Falls where she was treated for her injuries during the next several weeks and eventually released.

Analysis

Matthew Neuner and Elizabeth Dyer successfully completed a one-day, winter ascent of a difficult, technical mixed route on the south side of the Grand Teton. They were late completing the climb and elected to bivouac near the summit of the peak. During the descent Dyer slipped, was not able to perform a self-arrest, and consequently fell several hundred feet down the mountain. She was wearing a ski helmet, which was apparently destroyed during the fall, but probably saved her life. This particular accident illustrates the most common type of accident that occurs in the backcountry of Grand Teton National Park—a fall on snow and a failure to execute a successful self-arrest. (Source: Renny Jackson, SAR Incident Commander)

FALL ON ROCK, CLIMBING ALONE AND UNROPED
Wyoming, Grand Teton National Park, The Grand Traverse

On July 19 about 1030, I received a call from Fred of Butte, Montana. Fred voiced concern for a friend and climbing partner of his, Dwight Bishop (49), whom he believed was overdue from a climb of the Grand Traverse.

Fred was concerned because he thought that his friend had left on July 16 and that he thought that Bishop had intended to accomplish the traverse in one day. After confirming that Bishop's car was still at the Lupine Meadows trailhead, I initiated what was to become a very sizable search effort.

I began an interview with Fred Donich at about 1030. Donich noted that he thought that Bishop had left for the Traverse as early as some time Thursday morning (7/15) as he knew that the climber had contacted his mother by cell phone at that time. Donich believed that he could have left after that and that he might have taken bivouac equipment. He also thought that Bishop had probably taken a rope with him. Donich felt that the rope, however, would only be used to rappel certain sections of the climb that are easier to descend that way as opposed to the down-climbing alternative. Donich felt that Bishop would not use the rope to belay more difficult portions of the route such as the North Ridge or the Italian Cracks. It was Donich's strong feeling that Bishop would simply free-solo these difficult sections, relying more on his technical abilities, and preferring speed over the slower, yet perhaps safer technique of roped soloing. Bishop's technical climbing abilities were considerable, however. Donich had climbed with him as recently as the week before when they had rock climbed in the Humbug Spires of Montana. Donich stated that Bishop's sport climbing prowess included a red point ability of 5.12+, using the Yosemite Decimal Scale of rating climbs. Bishop was an accomplished alpinist, having climbed some of the great north faces in the Alps including that of the north face of the Eiger and Walker Spur. He had extensive climbing experience in the Teton Range, having done many of the most difficult climbs, sometimes in winter. Bishop had apparently climbed the Grand Traverse ten or twelve years earlier and was planning a winter attempt on the route at some future date. Bishop was also a very fit individual having competed in the bicycle road race, Race Across America, in 1993 and in 2000.

The Grand Traverse. The Grand Teton and the peaks that comprise the heart of the range are linked together in a great 11-mile arc that forms the upper boundary of the north and south forks of Garnet Canyon. The climb of this great arc has come to be known among climbers as The Grand Traverse. Eleven summits are found along the way with ten of them rising above the 12,000 foot elevation. Over 25,000 feet of elevation is gained and lost during the course of the Traverse. The successful first traverse, accomplished by Richard Long, John Evans, and Allen Steck was completed on August 12, 1963. Since that time the climb has evolved in that climbers usually begin at the east face of Teewinot and proceed from north to south along the ridge crest to Nez Perce. This is more difficult in that it involves an ascent of the North Ridge of the Grand Teton, one of the classic alpine routes in the United States. The two well-known pitches on the climb, the Chockstone Chimney and the Slab Pitch, are considered to be the cruxes of the route and can be very difficult indeed if wet or icy. The Chockstone Chimney is rated 5.8 on the Yosemite Decimal scale and the Slab Pitch is rated 5.7. The Grand Traverse is a highly sought-after climbing objective. Popularized and made famous by the speedy, summertime exploits of Alex Lowe and Rolando Garibotti, as well as having received some attention lately in the climbing magazines, the Grand Traverse has a good deal of traffic on it during the main climbing season.

A significant search effort was begun, involving many people. On the second day, the search team comprised of rangers Bywater and Byerly were assigned the search segment that included the north side of the Grand Teton as well as the upper portions of the Grandstand. Their assignment was to climb from the Lower Saddle to the Upper Saddle, traverse out along the Owen-Spalding route to the Second Ledge of the north face and descend to the Grandstand by rappelling the Italian Cracks route on the north face. Once on the Grandstand they were to investigate the east and west sides of the Grandstand and then climb back up the North Ridge route, looking for clues along the way. During the day this assignment changed slightly in that we requested that they try and make their way down to the Camelback and other items that we had investigated from the air during the previous day. This proved too hazardous, both for them as well as for another team who was working up the east face of the Grandstand from the bottom. Therefore, we requested that Bywater and Byerly instead work their way over to the Gunsight Notch in order to try and take a look at the West Ledges route on Mount Owen as well as perhaps the west side of the Grandstand.

This proved to be the key to success for the entire search operation. While descending from Gunsight Notch down the couloir on the west side, they made voice contact with a climbing party at 1750 who were in the process of making their way up the west side of the Grandstand as an approach for a climb of the North Ridge of the Grand. They indicated that they had discovered a pack and that they had left it marked with a cairn. Items contained within the pack indicated that whomever it belonged to had quite possibly been on the Grand Traverse route. Bywater and Byerly climbed up to and located the pack at 1807. A short time later, at 1822, Dwight Bishop's body was spotted simultaneously from the air and by the climbing team on the ground.

Analysis

Dwight Bishop was an accomplished alpinist and strong rock climber who had many years of experience climbing not only in the Tetons but in other great ranges of the world. Bishop was also a very fit individual having participated in a number of significant bicycle road races during his lifetime. Sometime during July 16, Bishop fell to his death while climbing on the Grand Teton. The Grand Traverse, which was the climbing route that he was on when he died, was certainly within his capabilities and, in fact, had been ascended by

Bishop years before. He was committed to the climb of that particular route in his mind, at least, as evidenced by Fred Donich, his climbing partner of many years, as well as that of a Jenny Lake climbing ranger, with whom he had had a discussion a few days before in the Blacktail Butte climbing area parking lot. Donich indicated to me that he thought that Bishop would have likely been free-soloing as opposed to roped soloing. Donich also felt that he would have likely taken a rope to facilitate certain portions of the route, such as the descent of Peak 11,840+, the first obstacle between the plateau to the west of Teewinot and the traverse over to Mount Owen. It was presumably Bishop's intention to get a very early start on the 16th, as evidenced by the fact that his alarm clock, which was found in his vehicle, was set for 2:00 a.m. Also found in the vehicle were a pair of crampons that Bishop had presumably left behind on the day of the climb.

Based on all of the information, it is likely that Bishop was free-soloing when he fell. Derived from photographs obtained during an aerial reconnaissance conducted the day after the recovery operation, it is also likely that Bishop fell from somewhere on the North Ridge route of the Grand Teton. The North Ridge route, as opposed to the "Italian Cracks," is the classic route of ascent of the Grand Teton during the course of a Grand Traverse climb. If Bishop fell from anywhere above the top of the normal second pitch of the North Ridge route, it is highly probably that he would end up on the west side of the Grandstand, which was indeed where he was found.

The free-soloist sacrifices the safety that is normally afforded the climber who is belaying or who is being belayed by a partner, for a lighter-weight and swifter style of climbing that has its own set of unique advantages. However, if anything goes wrong, the results are usually catastrophic. A momentary distraction, a hand or foot hold breaking, a slip on an unnoticed wet or icy spot, or an objective hazard such as rockfall, can all contribute to a loss of the all important focus that the free-soloist relies upon for success. (Source: Renny Jackson, SAR Incident Commander)

FALLING ROCK AND SLIP ON SNOW—UNABLE TO SELF-ARREST DUE TO INADEQUATE CLOTHING AND EQUIPMENT AND INEXPERIENCE
Wyoming, Grand Teton National Park, Middle Teton and Disappointment Peak

On July 28th, rangers made two rescues of injured parties—one from a point between Middle Teton and South Teton, the other from Disappointment Peak. The first occurred on Wednesday morning. Mysha Miskin (30) of Rexburg, Idaho, had been hit by falling rocks around 5:00 p.m. the previous evening while climbing the Chouinard Ridge on the Middle Teton with her husband, Garon Miskin. Although Mysha was injured by a rock that struck her just below the back of her climbing helmet, she and Garon continued to climb and summit the Middle Teton so that they could safely descend an easier route via the Southwest Couloir on the Middle Teton. By the time the climbers reached a point just below the saddle between Middle Teton and South Teton, Mysha was not able to continue. Garon hiked back up to the saddle and made a 911 call for assistance late Tuesday evening. Two rangers with emergency medical gear began hiking from Lupine Meadows trailhead into the South Fork of Garnet Canyon within an hour of the emergency call and reached Mysha at about 2:45 a.m. on Wednesday morning. Four other rangers packed in extra medical equipment and camping gear to care for the injured Mysha until the park's contract helicopter could fly with early morning light.

On Wednesday morning, the rangers carried Mysha by hand-litter to a helicopter landing spot just east of the Middle and South Teton saddle. She was flown out, then taken to St. John's Medical Center in Jackson for treatment of her injuries. Garon applied emergency first aid to his wife and the two climbers practiced good self rescue procedures until park rangers could reach them. They were well prepared for their climbing excursion and had extra clothing and rain gear with them.

The second helicopter-assisted rescue and evacuation took place at 4:30 p.m. Elizabeth Messaros (22) dislocated her shoulder while attempting to stop herself from sliding after she slipped on hard-packed snow in the Spoon Couloir on Disappointment Peak. Messaros slid about 150 feet before running into rocks and sustaining additional injuries. Teton Interagency dispatch received a cell phone call from Messaros' hiking partner Steve about 11:40 a.m. Rangers were just completing the transfer of equipment and rescue personnel from the South Fork of Garnet Canyon after the morning evacuation. The park's contract helicopter shuttled six rangers to a landing spot on the flanks of Disappointment Peak near the Grand Teton. The rangers then descended the Spoon Couloir, provided emergency medical care to Messaros, and lowered her to the bottom of the couloir after placing her in a climbing harness affixed to ropes. They helped Messaros walk to a spot just above Amphitheater Lake, where the helicopter landed and picked her up for a flight to the Lupine Meadows rescue facility. Messaros was then transferred to a park ambulance and transported to St. John's Medical Center for treatment of her injuries. Messaros was wearing tennis shoes and using ski poles, rather than an ice ax, at the time of the accident. (Source: From an NPS Morning report submitted by Jackie Skaggs, Public Affairs Specialist)

Analysis

Two contrasting stories. As for the latter, Ranger Renny Jackson said it above in the March 12 incident: Loss of control in a slide on snow is the most common incident in the park, and usually involves the lack of proper gear. (Source: Jed Williamson)

STATISTICAL TABLES

TABLE I
REPORTED MOUNTAINEERING ACCIDENTS

	Number of Accidents Reported		Total Persons Involved		Injured		Fatalities	
	USA	CAN	USA	CAN	USA	CAN	USA	CAN
1951	15		22		11		3	
1952	31		35		17		13	
1953	24		27		12		12	
1954	31		41		31		8	
1955	34		39		28		6	
1956	46		72		54		13	
1957	45		53		28		18	
1958	32		39		23		11	
1959	42	2	56	2	31	0	19	2
1960	47	4	64	12	37	8	19	4
1961	49	9	61	14	45	10	14	4
1962	71	1	90	1	64	0	19	1
1963	68	11	79	12	47	10	19	2
1964	53	11	65	16	44	10	14	3
1965	72	0	90	0	59	0	21	0
1966	67	7	80	9	52	6	16	3
1967	74	10	110	14	63	7	33	5
1968	70	13	87	19	43	12	27	5
1969	94	11	125	17	66	9	29	2
1970	129	11	174	11	88	5	15	5
1971	110	17	138	29	76	11	31	7
1972	141	29	184	42	98	17	49	13
1973	108	6	131	6	85	4	36	2
1974	96	7	177	50	75	1	26	5
1975	78	7	158	22	66	8	19	2
1976	137	16	303	31	210	9	53	6
1977	121	30	277	49	106	21	32	11
1978	118	17	221	19	85	6	42	10
1979	100	36	137	54	83	17	40	19
1980	191	29	295	85	124	26	33	8
1981	97	43	223	119	80	39	39	6
1982	140	48	305	126	120	43	24	14
1983	187	29	442	76	169	26	37	7
1984	182	26	459	63	174	15	26	6
1985	195	27	403	62	190	22	17	3
1986	203	31	406	80	182	25	37	14

	Number of Accidents Reported		Total Persons Involved		Injured		Fatalities	
	USA	CAN	USA	CAN	USA	CAN	USA	CAN
1987	192	25	377	79	140	23	32	9
1988	156	18	288	44	155	18	24	4
1989	141	18	272	36	124	11	17	9
1990	136	25	245	50	125	24	24	4
1991	169	20	302	66	147	11	18	6
1992	175	17	351	45	144	11	43	6
1993	132	27	274	50	121	17	21	1
1994	158	25	335	58	131	25	27	5
1995	168	24	353	50	134	18	37	7
1996	139	28	261	59	100	16	31	6
1997	158	35	323	87	148	24	31	13
1998	138	24	281	55	138	18	20	1
1999	123	29	248	69	91	20	17	10
2000	150	23	301	36	121	23	24	7
2001	150	22	276	47	138	14	16	2
2002	139	27	295	29	105	23	34	6
2003	118	29	231	32	105	22	18	6
2004	160	35	311	30	140	16	35	14
TOTALS	6,000	939	10,992	1962	5,073	701	1339	285

(Editor's Note: The totals for these columns have been incorrect from 1981. The individual years have been correct, but the totals went awry, resulting in an understatement of from four to over 300, except for total fatalities in Canada, the total of which was overstated by nine. The totals are now corrected. However, if the totals for Table II were added, they would not jibe with this table either. Vexatious, maybe irrelevant.)

TABLE II

Geographical Districts	1951–2003			2004		
	Number of Accidents	Deaths	Total Persons Involved	Number of Accidents	Deaths	Total Persons Involved
CANADA						
Alberta	490	134	1022	24	8	11
British Columbia	299	110	627	8	4	14
Yukon Territory	34	26	75	1	1	2
New Brunswick	1	0	0	0	0	0
Ontario	37	9	67	0	0	0
Quebec	29	9	60	2	1	3
East Arctic	8	2	21	0	0	0
West Arctic	1	1	2	0	0	0
Practice Cliffs[1]	20	2	36	0	0	0
UNITED STATES						
Alaska	461	173	766	11	2	37
Arizona, Nevada Texas	79	16	146	5	1	7
Atlantic–North	855	140	1493	31	4	56
Atlantic–South	86	23	153	6	0	12
California	1,134	269	2,331	42	10	75
Central	131	16	211	1	0	3
Colorado	707	196	2236	11	3	18
Montana, Idaho South Dakota	76	30	120	1	1	2
Oregon	173	99	404	12	3	22
Utah, New Mexico	141	53	264	15	4	24
Washington	983	303	796	18	5	35
Wyoming	519	117	962	10	4	35

[1]This category includes bouldering, artificial climbing walls, buildings, and so forth. These are also added to the count of each province, but not to the total count, though that error has been made in previous years. The Practice Cliffs category has been removed from the U.S. data.

TABLE III

	1951–03 USA	1959–03 CAN.	2004 USA	2004 CAN.
Terrain				
Rock	4141	503	96	18
Snow	2289	341	46	5
Ice	231	146	18	12
River	14	3	0	0
Unknown	22	9	0	0
Ascent or Descent				
Ascent	2735	555	118	23
Descent	2152	352	40	10
Unknown	247	10	1	2
Other[N.B.]	6	0	1	0
Immediate Cause				
Fall or slip on rock	2887	273	71	10
Slip on snow or ice	915	198	35	7
Falling rock, ice, or object	585	131	16	4
Exceeding abilities	500	29	25	1
Illness[1]	357	25	5	1
Stranded	310	49	13	3
Avalanche	276	120	2	5
Exposure	257	13	7	0
Rappel Failure/Error[2]	252	44	11	1
Loss of control/glissade	185	16	7	0
Nut/chock pulled out	183	8	8	1
Failure to follow route	164	29	7	0
Fall into crevasse/moat	152	48	1	2
Piton/ice screw pulled out	87	12	7	0
Faulty use of crampons	87	5	5	0
Lightning	45	7	1	0
Skiing[3]	50	10	1	1
Ascending too fast	61	0	3	0
Equipment failure	13	3	1	0
Other[4]	358	34	27	1
Unknown	60	9	1	0
Contributory Causes				
Climbing unroped	960	161	19	2
Exceeding abilities	877	199	4	1
Placed no/inadequate protection	646	94	27	2
Inadequate equipment/clothing	630	68	21	0
Weather	442	63	10	1
Climbing alone	370	67	13	2
No hard hat	304	28	12	1

	1951–03 USA	1959–03 CAN	2004 USA	2004 CAN
Contributory Causes (continued)				
Nut/chock pulled out	196	31	0	1
Inadequate belay	181	27	9	1
Darkness	134	20	2	0
Poor position	151	20	6	0
Party separated	110	10	3	2
Piton/ice screw pulled out	86	13	0	0
Failure to test holds	89	28	4	3
Exposure	57	13	0	0
Failed to follow directions	71	11	0	0
Illness1	39	9	0	0
Equipment failure	11	7	0	0
Other[4]	251	99	5	1
Age of Individuals				
Under 15	123	12	2	0
15-20	1226	202	9	1
21-25	1304	246	33	5
26-30	1208	205	27	3
31-35	1011	110	18	2
36-50	1090	136	58	5
Over 50	191	27	15	2
Unknown	1900	504	33	13
Experience Level				
None/Little	1676	294	48	5
Moderate (1 to 3 years)	1494	354	50	0
Experienced	1718	427	79	6
Unknown	1915	511	43	24
Month of Year				
January	202	23	7	2
February	196	51	2	4
March	279	66	13	2
April	381	33	8	5
May	847	55	18	2
June	979	65	30	4
July	1061	244	24	6
August	987	177	15	4
September	1136	70	11	4
October	415	38	20	0
November	175	14	5	2
December	86	24	7	0
Unknown	17	1	0	0
Type of Injury/Illness (Data since 1984)				
Fracture	1049	206	67	10
Laceration	622	71	35	0

	1951–03 USA	1959–03 CAN	2004 USA	2004 CAN
Type of Injury/Illness (Data since 1984) (continued)				
Abrasion	299	75	10	1
Bruise	406	77	27	4
Sprain/strain	281	29	24	2
Concussion	201	28	13	0
Hypothermia	144	15	3	1
Frostbite	112	9	4	0
Dislocation	99	15	10	1
Puncture	42	13	1	0
Acute Mountain Sickness	39	0	1	0
HAPE	65	0	1	0
HACE	23	0	0	0
Other[5]	274	43	20	4
None	184	182	23	6

[N.B.] Some accidents happen when climbers are at the top or bottom of a route, not climbing. They may be setting up a belay or rappel or are just not anchored when they fall. (This category created in 2001. We still have "Unknown" because of solo climbers.)

[1]These illnesses/injuries, which led directly or indirectly to the accident, included: AMS, deep vein thrombosis, tooth problems, HAPE, frostbite, and an acute abdomen.

[2]These include no back-up-knot—so rappelled off end of ropes, inadequate anchors, rope too short, improper use of descending device, inattention by belayer when lowering.

[3]This category was set up originally for ski mountaineering. Backcountry touring or snowshoeing incidents—even if one gets avalanched—are not in the data.

[4]These include: hand or foothold broke off (10); frostbite (3); unable to self-arrest (7); rope ascender came off; failure to disclose medical condition to guides (2); dislocated shoulder while mantling; rope jammed in crack; carrying ice ax upside down; bee attack; simul-climbing—so too much slack in rope; ice pillar broke off; threw whole rope down—so stranded; let go of ice tools; tied webbing knot incorrectly on rappel anchor—so came undone when weighted; late starts resulting in benighting (2); failure to follow instincts; wet rock (3); leader unable to communicate with belayer (2).

[5]These included: dehydration and exhaustion (5), DVT, rope burns on hands; kidney failure; collapsed lung; pneumo/hemothorax; heat exhaustion; multiple bee stings; internal injuries; acute abdomen (unknown problem); tooth problems; lightning burns.

(Editor's Note: Under the category "other," many of the particular items will have been recorded under a general category. For example, the climber who dislodges a rock that falls on another climber would be coded as Falling Rock/Object, or the climber who has a hand hold come loose and falls would also be coded as Fall On Rock.

A climber disappeared on Mt. Sir Sanford, but no details are known as to whether it was on ascent or descent or what the cause may have been so it is reported as "unknown.")

MOUNTAIN RESCUE UNITS IN NORTH AMERICA
**Denotes team fully certified—Technical Rock,
Snow & Ice, Wilderness Search;
S, R, SI = certified partially in Search, Rock, and/or Snow & Ice

ALASKA
Alaska Mountain Rescue Group. PO Box 241102, Anchorage,
AK 99524. www.amrg.org
Denali National Park SAR. PO Box 588, Talkeetna, AK 99676.
Dena_talkeetna@nps.gov
US Army Alaskan Warfare Training Center. #2900 501 Second St., APO AP 96508

ARIZONA
Apache Rescue Team. PO Box 100, St. Johns, AZ 85936
Arizona Department Of Public Safety Air Rescue. Phoenix, Flagstaff, Tucson,
Kingman, AZ
Arizona Division Of Emergency Services. Phoenix, AZ
Grand Canyon National Park Rescue Team. PO Box 129, Grand Canyon, AZ 86023
**Central Arizona Mountain Rescue Team/Maricopa County Sheriff's Office
MR.** PO Box 4004 Phoenix, AZ 85030. www.mcsomr.org
Sedona Fire District Special Operations Rescue Team. 2860 Southwest Dr.,
Sedona, AZ 86336. ropes@sedona.net
Southern Arizona Rescue Assn/Pima County Sheriff's Office. PO Box 12892,
Tucson, AZ 85732. http://hambox.theriver.com/sarci/sara01.html

CALIFORNIA
Altadena Mountain Rescue Team. 780 E. Altadena Dr., Altadena, CA 91001
www.altadenasheriffs.org/rescue/amrt.html
Bay Area Mountain Rescue Team. PO Box 19184, Stanford, CA 94309
bamru@hooked.net
California Office of Emergency Services. 2800 Meadowview Rd., Sacramento, CA.
95832. warning.center@oes.ca.gov
China Lake Mountain Rescue Group. PO Box 2037, Ridgecrest, CA 93556
www.clmrg.org
Inyo County Sheriff's Posse SAR. PO Box 982, Bishop, CA 93514
inyocosar@juno.com
Joshua Tree National Park SAR. 74485 National Monument Drive,
Twenty Nine Palms, CA 92277. patrick_suddath@nps.gov
Los Padres SAR Team. PO Box 6602, Santa Barbara, CA 93160-6602
Malibu Mountain Rescue Team. PO Box 222, Malibu, CA 90265.
www.mmrt.org
Montrose SAR Team. PO Box 404, Montrose, CA 91021
Riverside Mountain Rescue Unit. PO Box 5444, Riverside,
CA 92517. www.rmru.org   rmru@bigfoot.com
San Bernardino County Sheriff's Cave Rescue Team. 655 E. Third St.
San Bernardino, CA 92415
www.sbsd-vfu.org/units/SAR/SAR203/sar203_1.htm
San Bernardino County So/ West Valley SAR. 13843 Peyton Dr., Chino Hills, CA
91709.

**San Diego Mountain Rescue Team. PO Box 81602, San Diego, CA 92138. www.sdmrt.org

**San Dimas Mountain Rescue Team. PO Box 35, San Dimas, CA 91773

**Santa Clarita Valley SAR / L.A.S.O. 23740 Magic Mountain Parkway, Valencia, CA 91355. http://members.tripod.com/scvrescue/

Sequoia-Kings Canyon National Park Rescue Team. Three Rivers, CA 93271

**Sierra Madre SAR. PO Box 24, Sierra Madre, CA 91025. www.mra.org/smsrt.html

**Ventura County SAR. 2101 E. Olson Rd, Thousand Oaks, CA 91362 www.vcsar.org

Yosemite National Park Rescue Team. PO Box 577-SAR, Yosemite National Park, CA 95389

COLORADO

**Alpine Rescue Team. PO Box 934, Evergreen, CO 80439 www.heart-beat-of-evergreen.com/alpine/alpine.html

Colorado Ground SAR. 2391 Ash St, Denver, CO 80222 www.coloradowingcap.org/CGSART/Default.htm

**Crested Butte SAR. PO Box 485, Crested Butte, CO 81224

Douglas County Search And Rescue. PO Box 1102, Castle Rock, CO 80104. www.dcsarco.org info@dcsarco.org

**El Paso County SAR. 3950 Interpark Dr, Colorado Springs, CO 80907-9028. www.epcsar.org

Eldorado Canyon State Park. PO Box B, Eldorado Springs, CO 80025

**Grand County SAR. Box 172, Winter Park, CO 80482

**Larimer County SAR. 1303 N. Shields St., Fort Collins, CO 80524. www.fortnet.org/LCSAR/ lcsar@co.larimer.co.us

**Mountain Rescue Aspen. 630 W. Main St, Aspen, CO 81611 www.mountainrescueaspen.org

Park County SAR, CO. PO Box 721, Fairplay, CO 80440

Rocky Mountain National Park Rescue Team. Estes Park, CO 80517

**Rocky Mountain Rescue Group. PO Box Y, Boulder, CO 80306 www.colorado.edu/StudentGroups/rmrg/ rmrg@colorado.edu

Routt County SAR. PO Box 772837, Steamboat Springs, CO 80477 RCSAR@co.routt.co.us

**Summit County Rescue Group. PO Box 1794, Breckenridge, CO 80424

**Vail Mountain Rescue Group. PO Box 1597, Vail, CO 81658 http://sites.netscape.net/vailmra/homepage vmrg@vail.net

**Western State College Mountain Rescue Team. Western State College Union, Gunnison, CO 81231. org_mrt@western.edu

IDAHO

**Bonneville County SAR. 605 N. Capital Ave, Idaho Falls, ID 83402 www.srv.net/~jrcase/bcsar.html

**Idaho Mountain SAR. PO Box 741, Boise, ID 83701. www.imsaru.org rsksearch@aol.com

MAINE

Acadia National Park SAR. Bar Harbor, Maine

MARYLAND
Maryland Sar Group. 5434 Vantage Point Road, Columbia, MD 21044
Peter_McCabe@Ed.gov

MONTANA
Glacier National Park SAR. PO Box 423, Glacier National Park,
West Glacier, MT 59936

Northwest Montana Regional SAR Assn. c/o Flat County SO,
800 S. Main, Kalispell, MT 59901

Western Montana Mountain Rescue Team. University of Montana,
University Center—Rm 105 Missoula, MT 59812

NEVADA
Las Vegas Metro PD SAR. 4810 Las Vegas Blvd., South Las Vegas,
NV 89119. www.lvmpdsar.com

NEW MEXICO
Albuquerque Mountain Rescue Council. PO Box 53396, Albuquerque,
NM 87153. www.abq.com/amrc/ albrescu@swcp.com

NEW HAMPSHIRE
Appalachian Mountain Club. Pinkham Notch Camp, Gorham, NH 03581
Mountain Rescue Service. PO Box 494, North Conway, NH 03860

NEW YORK
76 SAR. 243 Old Quarry Rd., Feura Bush, NY 12067
Mohonk Preserve Rangers. PO Box 715, New Paltz, NY 12561
NY State Forest Rangers. 50 Wolf Rd., Room 440C, Albany, NY 12233

OREGON
Corvallis Mountain Rescue Unit. PO Box 116, Corvallis, OR 97339
www.cmrv.peak.org

(S, R) **Deschutes County SAR**. 63333 West Highway 20, Bend, OR 97701

Eugene Mountain Rescue. PO Box 20, Eugene, OR 97440

Hood River Crag Rats Rescue Team. 2880 Thomsen Rd., Hood River,
OR 97031

Portland Mountain Rescue. PO Box 5391, Portland, OR 97228
www.pmru.org info@pmru.org

PENNSYLVANNIA
Allegheny Mountain Rescue Group. c/o Mercy Hospital,
1400 Locust, Pittsburgh, PA 15219. www.asrc.net/amrg

Wilderness Emergency Strike Team. 11 North Duke Street, Lancaster,
PA 17602. www.west610.org

UTAH
Davis County Sheriff's SAR. PO Box 800, Farmington, UT 84025
www.dcsar.org

Rocky Mountain Rescue Dogs. 3353 S. Main #122, Salt Lake City, UT 84115

Salt Lake County Sheriff's SAR. 3510 South 700 West, Salt Lake City, UT 84119

San Juan County Emergency Services. PO Box 9, Monticello, UT 84539
**Utah County Sherrif's SAR. PO Box 330, Provo, UT 84603.
ucsar@utah.uswest.net
**Weber County Sheriff's Mountain Rescue. 745 Nancy Dr, Ogden,
UT 84403. http://planet.weber.edu/mru
Zion National Park SAR. Springdale, UT 84767

VERMONT
**Stowe Hazardous Terrain Evacuation. P.O. Box 291, Stowe, VT 05672
www.stowevt.org/htt/

VIRGINIA
Air Force Rescue Coordination Center. Suite 101, 205 Dodd Building,
Langley AFB, VA 23665. www2.acc.af.mil/afrcc/airforce.rescue@usa.net

WASHINGTON STATE
**Bellingham Mountain Rescue Council. PO Box 292, Bellingham, WA 98225
**Central Washington Mountain Rescue Council. PO Box 2663, Yakima, WA
98907. www.nwinfo.net/~cwmr/ cwmr@nwinfo.net
**Everett Mountain Rescue Unit. PO Box 2566, Everett, WA 98203
emrui@aol.com
Mount Rainier National Park Rescue Team. Longmire, WA 98397
North Cascades National Park Rescue Team. 728 Ranger Station Rd,
Marblemount, WA 98267
**Olympic Mountain Rescue. PO Box 4244, Bremerton, WA 98312
www.olympicmountainrescue.org information@olympicmountainrescue.org
Olympic National Park Rescue Team. 600 Park Ave, Port Angeles, WA 98362
**Seattle Mountain Rescue. PO Box 67, Seattle, WA 98111
www.eskimo.com/~pc22/SMR/smr.html
**Skagit Mountain Rescue. PO Box 2, Mt. Vernon, WA 98273
**Tacoma Mountain Rescue. PO Box 696, Tacoma, WA 98401
www.tmru.org
North Country Volcano Rescue Team. 404 S. Parcel Ave, Yacolt, WA 98675
www.northcountryems.org/vrt/index.html

WASHINGTON, DC
National Park Service, EMS/SAR Division. Washington, DC
US Park Police Aviation. Washington, DC

WYOMING
Grand Teton National Park Rescue Team. PO Box 67, Moose, WY 83012
Park County SAR, WY. Park County SO, 1131 11th, Cody, WY 82412

CANADA
North Shore Rescue Team. 147 E. 14th St, North Vancouver, B.C.,
Canada V7L 2N4
**Rocky Mountain House SAR. Box 1888, Rocky Mountain House, Alberta,
Canada T0M 1T0

MOUNTAIN RESCUE ASSOCIATION

PO Box 880868
San Diego, CA 92168-0868
www.mra.org • www.mountainrescuehonorguard.org

Monty Bell, President/CEO
San Diego Mountain Rescue Team, CA
ubs@att/net
619-884-9456

Fran Martoglio, Vice President
Tacoma Mountain Rescue Unit, WA
thegirlpilot@hotmail.com
360-482-6190

Kayley Trujillo, Secretary-Treasurer/CFO
San Diego Mountain Rescue Unit, CA
kayley@kayley.net

Neil Van Dyke, Officer/Member at Large
Stowe Hazardous Terrain Evacuation, VT
neilvd@stoweagle.com

Tim Kovacs, Public Affairs Director/PIO, Past President
Central AZ Mountain Rescue/Maricopa County SO MR, AZ
tkovacs@cox.net
602-819-4066

Charley Shimanski, Education Director/Office Member at Large
Alpine Rescue Team, CO
shimanski@speedtrail.net
303-384-0110 x11

Dr. Ken Zafren, MD, FACEP, Medical Chair
Alaska Mountain Rescue Group, AK
zafren@alaska.net

Dan Hourihan, Immediate Past President
Alaska Mountain Rescue Group, AK
danh@dnr.state.ak.us